Praise for
Dented Cans and Classic Cars

"Enjoyed the book very much. I laughed at the humorous comments. Great information to consider while deciding on future moves while downsizing. I hope the author continues with more adventures."

—Janet Aggen, speech teacher

"I always look forward to another Dan Krause book, and I was not disappointed with his latest. He takes us on a journey many of us will have to face as we age—finding a place to live out our golden years. It is a wise, compassionate, and thought-provoking trip presented in a clear, concise, and intelligent manner—heavily laced with Krause's signature humor. I recommend this book to anyone, especially those facing this type of decision for themselves or someone they love or for anyone who just needs some good laughs."

—David Countryman, special education teacher

"Buy the book, but use a yellow highlighter so you can read the numerous LOL sentences to your friends (or your enemies)! BTW, face facts: we are all dented cans."

—David Edelberg, MD, author of *The Triple Whammy*

"Read this book if you are moving. Read this book if you are not moving. Mr. Krause is insightful, humorous, and sometimes biting. You will enjoy your conversation with him."

—Paul Mooradian, a new condo dweller

Dented Cans and Classic Cars:
Reflections on a Retirement Community
by Daniel Krause

© Copyright 2024 Daniel Krause

ISBN 979-8-88824-412-8

All rights reserved. No part of this publication may be reproduced, stored in a retrieval system, or transmitted in any form or by any means—electronic, mechanical, photocopy, recording, or any other—except for brief quotations in printed reviews, without the prior written permission of the author.

Published by

3705 Shore Drive
Virginia Beach, VA 23455
800-435-4811
www.koehlerbooks.com

Dented Cans and Classic Cars

Reflections on a Retirement Community

Daniel Krause

VIRGINIA BEACH
CAPE CHARLES

Table of Contents

Introduction 3

1: Why This Book? 5

2: The Big Decision! 25

3. Where Are We Going? 45

4: First Impressions of Our New Home 62

5: Our Long-Standing Marital Treaty: Now Null and Void! 82

6: The New Neighbors! 99

7: What the Hell Happened?* 117

8: Water Crisis at the Home! 127

9: A Few More Thoughts About Life at *the Home!* 137

Introduction

Wikipedia provides a good definition for "dented cans," which might be useful for Americans who never conceived of the idea that dented cans exist, let alone that they are sold in the nation's grocery stores. At least in some of them. I don't think you would ever see dented cans in a high-end grocery store; it would be like an elegant department store selling used clothing. Or maybe something like a Mercedes-Benz dealer with rusty pickup trucks on the lot.

Anyway, Wikipedia has useful details about dented cans: seams are on the side of the can and are usually covered by the label. End seams are on the top and bottom of the can. *If there is a dent over any of these seams, the can has a major defect, meaning it is unsafe.* If a dent has sharp or pointed edges, we can also consider the can to have an unsafe defect.

It is probably wise to skip any dented cans you find, and you should go back to the shelf for an undamaged one. On the other hand, if the dent is in the middle of the can and not near the seams, you can be comfortable buying and using the food.

I spent four years working in a Chicago grocery store that was located in a predominantly low-income community. Periodically, as I restocked the shelves and found, or somehow managed to create, damaged cans by my carelessness, I threw the dented containers into the cart we kept for such items. We had a sign on the cart: "Reduced for quick sale!" The cart was at the back of the store, and none of the cans had a price of more than ten cents. The cans always sold fast.

I learned that dented cans are not as valuable as those without any defects, even though the product is just as good—arguably similar to the way we evaluate our oldest citizens.

1.

Why This Book?

"For of all sad words of tongue or pen,
The saddest are these: 'It might have been!'"

—John Greenleaf Whittier

Curious individuals browsing through their bookstore's shelves and eventually finding this book might have a few questions: Why did he write this book? And why now? Why not wait a few more years until world events calm down? Will they ever calm down?

Anyway, at last count, if we believe Amazon, there are more than two million books currently in print. How many people are looking for another new book, even one that takes a somewhat different look at one of the country's major concerns?

This brings up another question: how many Americans read books with any regularity? Educated individuals seem to browse more than they read. The data show that about 60 percent of Americans read a book during the past year. That statistic doesn't seem bad, but this means that seventeen percent of Americans, our friends and neighbors, read *no* books during the past year. None!

You can be positive or negative about those percentages, but I put myself in the negative camp. I have a hard time understanding why so many presumably educated Americans do not read books on a regular basis. I understand that books are expensive unless you go to the "reduced" shelves in the bookstore, but we always have our public libraries. You will find any book you want on your public library's shelves. Or they will get it for you, depending on where you live.

Anyway, why am I throwing another book into this crowded marketplace? Well, this book is about America's older generation, and there should be readers anxious for more information about this age cohort. You remember them, the infamous baby boomers, the hippie crowd, the "draft beer, not people" gang, the make peace, not war group who intended to make their own clothes and live off the land, maybe raising a few chickens mostly for the eggs because who wants to butcher innocent chickens?

I don't have to tell you that things didn't quite work out, even with the chickens. But many Americans, me for example, are wondering what happened to those ambitious and admirable plans. Why are many boomers now having questions and concerns about where to live during the last segment of their lives and about what they should be doing with their spare time since very few of them are living off the land and harvesting eggs from their chickens?

Right now, they—and I suppose I should start saying "we" because I belong in this age group—seem to be having a hard time finding the most comfortable places to live out the so-called *golden years.*

Where are America's old people supposed to live? Are there explicit rules about age-based relocation? Why don't we stay where we are? What are we looking for when we move? And is anyone pushing us to move, with something sinister afoot, like desperate relatives trying to get Grandma into a home so they can sell her classic house for a small fortune? And while we are on the subject, who do younger Americans have in their minds when they talk about "old people?"

I got into this topic of "elderly housing" pretty much by accident. Accidents are a contributing factor to much that happens in our lives. In my life, anyway. Sometimes, accidents are the major force. We think we have a good idea of where we are heading, but something unexpected happens to deflect our interest, and we start moving, maybe even running full speed in a new direction. We can even forget where we were going before we started heading west instead of east until, maybe years later, we happen to look back and wonder, *What the hell was I thinking? Why didn't I follow my first plan and keep going east? Wouldn't I have been better off sticking with that first plan?*

But after you thought about it, maybe your first plan wasn't that good. That might explain why you got deflected. Or maybe that first idea was more of a vague idea than an actual planning document with well-defined categories and items to check off on a written list. In the last few years, telephones have mostly replaced paper planners, and society is the lesser for it. But by phone or paper, it is hard now to plan our lives with any precision. There are always events you don't anticipate, so it can be impossible to adhere to a plan you made months ago.

Are people depressed when they can't check off at least one item on their to-do list? I find it frustrating to ask a friend out for an impromptu dinner and watch him consulting his calendar before declining. Was an idea or plan from months ago a better idea than a dinner at a great restaurant with a two-for-one dinner special?

Earlier in my life, I didn't have any long-term plans, written or otherwise. I don't remember having any plans other than finishing what I was doing that week. Or even that day. Maybe I had a few vague plans for the coming weekend, like going to a movie with a girl I wanted to ask out, but beyond that? Long-term planning was not part of my life when I was nineteen! That may have been a mistake, but as with all the "what-ifs" in our lives, I will never know how things might have turned out. And not knowing is probably a good thing.

Anyway, that is how I ended up in the army at the tender age of nineteen. I had no plans after finishing two years of college and no money to continue my formal education. I moved into a more informal educational experience, which is not a bad way to describe army life. My army career was an occasionally frustrating but mostly interesting three-year span, filled with learning experiences I couldn't get from books.

I am sure that I gave the US Army their money's worth, and I probably did because, in those days, the army didn't pay much. But after three years, I was happy to receive my discharge, and I think they were happy to hand it to me. The reenlistment officer told me, and I think he was kidding, "I have to give you this reenlistment talk, but if you stay in the army, then I'm getting out."

After my discharge, I spent several months as a gas meter reader, easily one of our country's least appealing jobs. Lots of walking and climbing, and the pay was terrible. I took the position because I could start work the next day, and I needed money. That short span between the initial interview and starting work should have been a clue that this was not a job people stood in line for. Or keep for long.

Reading a meter is not difficult; my training involved about an hour of practice with a supervisor. "You are doing very well at this!"—a comment he probably made to every new employee—and then off you go with your hat, a flashlight, and a meter book where you record your findings that the gas company used to send out the monthly bills, usually with a warning that your gas would be turned off if you didn't pay within a specified period. Public utilities were not sympathetic organizations then. I don't think things have changed much.

My workday involved picking my way through a series of dark basements on Chicago's South Side, looking for the gas meters. The buildings usually had a meter for each apartment and were usually situated in the farthest basement corners, sometimes in places you wouldn't expect to find meters. I envisioned the construction guys laughing when they installed the meters underneath the building's washtubs. Or high on a wall where you needed a ladder to read them.

You eventually find the meters—although more than once, I never could—read the dials, carefully record your observations in the book—or you do if your flashlight still works and if the cobwebs are not too dense—and then you get the hell out, hoping there are no problems with a tenant who wonders what you are doing in their basement. The gas company had a uniform of sorts, not neat and military, like cops or soldiers, just gray shirts and caps that said "Gas Company." I did look somewhat official, but not like anyone empowered to make an arrest.

You won't find many good things in basements. At least, I never did. Apartment basements are places where tenants store strange collections like Barbie dolls or old magazines. They are not like home basements with rec rooms and places for kids to play. The lower levels of apartment buildings are dark, often dirty, and always sinister places that residents go only if they have to. Unless you are a meter reader.

My family lived in a series of Chicago apartments, and I never remember being asked to retrieve something from our basement. My family never had anything down there. From what I remember, none of the tenants did.

If I had to pick out a particularly bad moment in my basement meter-reading days, and there were more than a few, I think stepping on a dead animal had to be the low point. When my shoe (early in my meter reading career, I knew not to wear tennis shoes to work and chose heavy hiking boots) stepped on something soft, I thought it might be a pillow or a discarded mattress. Remember, it was dark down there. But when I aimed my flashlight and saw what I had stepped on, it was what was left of a dog. I think it was a dog. It could have been a raccoon or a large cat. I had no intention of taking a closer look.

I wondered at the time how the poor animal ended up there. *Was he left to starve in the basement, neglected by his owner?* That was a good possibility because South Chicago was not known as a dog-friendly community. *Or did the poor animal wander into that basement looking for food and warmth but found neither? Should I call someone?* Dead animals were not covered in my hour of formal training, so I left the basement without doing or saying anything. This was my first experience with the surprisingly instinctive and successful "don't ask, don't tell" philosophy. It worked for me that time. And for other times in my life.

But it is sad that the modern world has largely done away with meter readers. Meter reading is done automatically now, so there are no more meter readers walking into the nation's basements, yelling out a cheerful, "Gas man!" as they search for the elusive meters. Another American job category fades into history, along with horseshoeing, lamp lighting, and most newspaper stands. That was another job I had as a kid, selling papers from a wooden paper stand on a busy urban intersection.

Anyway, after three months spent wandering through the city's basements, I changed careers and went to work at what used to be called "the telephone company." This job change was another serendipitous experience because I had no intention of going to work for another public utility. But even early in my meter career, I would have done pretty much anything that involved getting away from those basements.

I was wandering around downtown Chicago, filling out applications at any office that accepted them, and my brother, who was also wandering in search of a better job, suggested that I go to the telephone company employment office because "they are hiring."

It might seem strange—and maybe unbelievable to a younger person who grew up with their own mobile phone—that there once was an organization known as the Telephone Company. Back in the iconic days of the 1960s, no one ever wondered what organization you had in mind when you made a remark about the telephone company. And it is fair to say that most of those remarks were positive.

Americans seemed to like their telephone company then. They might have been frustrated with it sometimes, but people could always count on the telephone company to deliver the important service at a reasonable rate. That was their job as a public utility, and they took that responsibility seriously.

AT&T was *the* telephone company in America, and their control over the nation's telephone service was complete and mostly unchallenged. There were occasional lawsuits about the company being a "monopoly," and of course it was, but that exclusiveness was not considered a problem. Except for a few isolated areas in the country, which AT&T didn't care much about anyway, there was no other telephone company for their captive customers. That is the way the nation's telephone system worked then, and for the most part, it worked fairly well.

But if you purchased a telephone instrument elsewhere, maybe at your local county fair, and tried to connect it to the Bell System, that could be a problem. The telephone company would know about the intrusion because they had their ways, and they would come after you. Or they would send guys like me to issue some threats.

On several occasions, I had to visit the homes or businesses of people who used unapproved, and not incidentally, unbilled, equipment. I felt uneasy, warning the violators that they faced severe consequences if they persisted; I have never been good at issuing ultimatums. And I was never sure what would happen if they refused to disconnect their illegal equipment.

A few times, I told the offenders that they could "lose their telephone service forever," but I don't think that would have happened. I couldn't imagine the telephone company cutting off service to a family with two young children because they were using an unlicensed telephone extension in the nursery. After the short talks, which I tried to make as pleasant as possible, I walked out with a warning to "be sure to disconnect that illegal extension" and left with a wink and a nod. And someday, someone will have to explain to me the meaning of "a wink and a nod."

Anyway, I enjoyed working for Ma Bell. She was a compassionate if somewhat impersonal employer, providing, among other benefits, a tuition remission program and a chance to purchase her stock at a discount. I never got too committed to that stock purchase plan because as soon as I had one share of AT&T stock in my portfolio, I sold it. I was on the low end of the company pay scale and had no room in my budget for savings. Or stock portfolios.

Ironically, the college classes gave me a new and unfamiliar sense of idealism and a desire to get more involved with the nation's social issues. Then, as now, there were plenty of issues to grapple with, and I wanted to grapple. These were new feelings for me because it is difficult to grow up with any idealism living on Chicago's South Side. That area has never been a springboard for idealism. Kids in my neighborhood mostly got jobs as policemen and firemen, not physicians or lawyers.

Anyway, I told myself that I shouldn't be sitting in a comfortable office chair worrying about telephone service and warning customers about unapproved equipment. I should be out in the world, curbing violence, ending the war, feeding the hungry, and housing the homeless. You could have a lot on your plate if you were issue-oriented in the 1960s. Sometimes I wish I would have told myself, *Why don't you just read a good book?*

Anyway, I changed direction again and threw out my plan, although I never had a definite plan. After consultations with my wife, who was already idealistic and didn't need any prodding, I quit my job at the telephone company and returned to school full-time.

What the hell was I thinking? Good question, and I wish someone had posed it to me then! If I could go back in time and talk to myself, I'd advise myself to think carefully about that resignation, that I might be jumping into a situation I didn't understand. If you remember that movie, *Peggy Sue Got Married*—and there is no reason you shouldn't if you enjoy provocative movies—I identified with Peggy Sue's motivation for a life reset. She was frustrated with her life, and depending on how you interpret the movie, she got it. I can't say I ever regretted going back to school.

Yes, I can! There were more good school days than bad ones, but the bad ones were painful. It is harder to sit through boring classes when you are older and more experienced. You also find it easier to distinguish a bad from a good classroom experience, and you are less willing to accept the bad times without voicing a complaint.

I can still remember university class sessions that were so boring, so stifling of creative thought and whatever innovative impulses I might have had that my mind wandered in directions that had nothing to do with the class material. Sometimes, trying to get through the tedium, I even pictured myself on one of those long army marches, thinking about walking under a hot sun in step with a hundred other guys. That should tell you how bad some of the classes were. Fondly remembering a long, hot march with a full pack on your back means you must be in a bad place.

I remember one class in particular; I wish I understood why our bad memories tend to be more persistent. Anyway, in this class, the professor spent the bulk of each session, two agonizing hours every week, reading the highlighted sentences in the assigned text. He read the sentences, never more than one or two; then, he would raise his eyes and ask in his dreary monotone, "Are there any questions on this point?"

Usually, there were no questions because most of the class was either asleep or had traveled to their personal private mental zones that had nothing to do with the book. Maybe some of my classmates were marching with me. I had the impression that the professor didn't want to be in that room any more than we did. Not incidentally, I received a D in this class.

So, there I was, battle-hardened after three years of military service, sensitized by my harrowing experiences within Chicago's dark basements, and energized by my work at the telephone company. After returning to school, I developed an interest in mental illness. Not in clinical treatments of the disease since sociology was my new major, and sociologists do not often get involved in clinical work. But I wanted to know more about the dynamics of mental disorders. Maybe I thought I would understand my own family's sometimes erratic behavior.

My family tree contains episodes of mental disorders. They found one of my uncles bricking himself into a secluded corner of his basement. If a neighbor hadn't come by to borrow a drill, my uncle could still be in that basement, unless he was lucky enough to have a conscientious meter reader. If not, everyone would be wondering what happened to Uncle Al. And he was one of my more stable uncles.

I wanted to understand what happened to people who were diagnosed with a mental disorder and sent to a full-care institution. State mental hospitals were more prevalent in past years. In virtually every state, you could find clusters of foreboding gray government buildings, often with bars or chain fencing over the windows and lining the grounds, the kinds of places that gave Charles Dickens nightmares. State mental institutions were like above-ground basements.

I was curious about these institutions. Did treatments in institutional settings help patients resume productive lives? Being in an institution for more than twenty years never helped my uncle, although he never tried the brick thing again. Jack Nicholson's classic performance in *One Flew Over The Cuckoo's Nest* vividly examined the issues involved in placing someone in an institution. One sad case in Illinois involved a man who was put in an institution and remained there for more than twenty years. It turned out that the "gibberish" the man was speaking, which was the reason for his confinement, was an obscure European dialect that no one understood.

I spent more than a year trying to establish precisely what society had in its mind with its medical designation of the "mentally ill." Precision, though, was not always evident in cases of involuntary institutionalization. I ran across a fascinating book by Thomas Szasz, *The Myth of Mental Illness*. The book changed my thinking, at least temporarily.

Szasz argued that there was no such thing as mental illness, that the designation was more of a political than a medical diagnosis and was applied to people who did not fit into the prevailing social structures. You can guess what reading that book did to my interest in mental illnesses. According to Szasz, mental illness was simply a modern type of witchcraft.

But I was still interested in full-care institutions and how they affected patient behavior. The college town we lived in then had no mental institutions, other than the university dormitories, so I decided to do a research project in a local nursing home. The home was a full-care institution and provided a great laboratory to look at the question of how institutions affected behavior. And the local administrators let me inside the building, access no researcher can take for granted. People don't like to work or even relax while researchers are walking around with notebooks and pencils. Who would blame them? But to make this long story short, that is how I got into the topic of elderly housing.

That interest in full-care institutions led me to another line of research, what sociologists describe as social ecology. This perspective examines the effect of structures on human behavior. Winston Churchill summarized the approach. "We shape our buildings; thereafter they shape us." I was never sure if Churchill meant that this as a description or a warning. But the Brits have a knack for producing political leaders who speak in memorable phrases.

Back to the nursing home! I was fascinated, looking at the way the older people in that institution reacted to their structured living arrangements. At first, it was a little unnerving, watching senior citizens being directed during the day as though they were school children. I remember one administrator explaining to me why their institution served five meals a day. "It's a great system with our mealtimes; our people are always coming or going to a meal. It keeps them occupied."

This administrator was a kind man, trained in nursing home administration, but that condescending approach struck me as wrong on many levels. It still does, although from what I can tell, the institutional thinking has changed. For one thing, I haven't run into another place that serves five meals a day.

As recently as the 1970s, options for elderly housing were limited, especially if older people had to consider costs. Most people did, and still do. You lived in your home and stayed there until you couldn't, until you could not accomplish the "activities of daily living." If you couldn't rely on your family or friends or neighbors for support with your daily essential tasks, then you moved to a nursing home. You did the best you could with the activities of daily living for as long as you could because the alternative was frightening. Then, as now, Americans were terrified of "being forced into a nursing home."

If older people moved from their own homes to an apartment, problems with handling daily chores might not be as evident. But problems could still emerge. Older people living in high-rise apartments might not be able to make the trip to the building trash room or get to a grocery store, and they store garbage in their homes until the smell prompts the neighbors to call the authorities.

And that was life for older citizens. Either you lived in your home or apartment and kept it presentable, or someone noticed, and the authorities moved you to an institution, usually with you protesting the whole way. There weren't many midpoints for older Americans.

One possible midpoint for older people, at least if they lived in a big city, involved SROs (single room occupancy) establishments. These buildings were mostly outdated hotels that had been modified to provide affordable housing for older people. No one wanted to maintain the buildings as hotels because of the financial outlay. But they didn't have to put in much money to use the buildings for elderly housing. SROs were a win-win for the major players, depending on how you define winning. And how you defined "major players."

The SRO rooms were what you might expect from an old hotel—small rooms with even smaller bathrooms, situated along a series of dreary hallways. There were no kitchens in the rooms, but most places allowed residents to have hot plates and apartment-sized refrigerators. If I had to use one word to describe the apartments, it would be "drab" or maybe "depressing."

SRO residents sometimes found local establishments that served subsidized lunches or dinners. Sometimes, the SROs themselves would make subsidized meals available on-site for their residents, and that serving would be the major meal of the residents' days. Funding came from federal or state funds. I had the chance to eat one of the meals, and with three years of experience with army food, I was prepared for the bland meals.

The rents were affordable, but social services were pretty much nonexistent. If the SRO was in a good neighborhood, residents might have a park close by to feed pigeons, play chess, or people-watch. In general, an SRO might have been better than a nursing home because it was your "own place," but depending on your needs, it may not have been much better.

A French organization, The Little Brothers of the Poor, established a branch in Chicago in 1959. What fascinated me about this organization was its philosophy that "nurturing the soul" is as important as feeding the body. "Flowers before bread" was their motto. That is a great organizational motto!

Their home-delivered meals permitted a lot of older Chicagoans to stay in their homes. Their innovative program was the catalyst for more municipalities to offer elderly home-delivered meal services. The Little Brothers food was not bad, in part because it often came with a small bottle of good wine. Remember, I said, "Good wine."

But then, as now, moving to a nursing home represented a perceived failure for everyone involved. Older people did not want to be placed in an institution because they would lose their independence. Families did not like the idea of putting Mom or Dad into "a home" because they knew that their parents did not want to go, and there was a stigma associated with "putting your parents into a home." But there may be no other option.

Even if the family has an extra room, bringing another generation into a home could end up a problem for everyone. Especially if Mom or Dad had their own ideas about how the household should operate. Contemporary families often have existing problems. Bringing either spouse's parents into an already stressed home can be the final straw that tears a family apart.

And then there is the issue of the physical care that the family might not be trained or able to provide. If the older person needs help with administering medication, food preparation, going to the toilet, or bathing, family members might not be equipped or inclined to handle that demanding caregiver work. And finally, the costs of maintaining an older family member in the home could be prohibitive. There are some good reasons why an older person might not fit into their son's or daughter's home and why a nursing home may be the best of some bad options.

A few years ago, big cities began experiencing a phenomenon with the picturesque designation "dropping Granny." There were variations, but the story unfolded along the following lines. The older person lived in her son's house for a period of time, maybe several years. The living situation was difficult, with frayed tempers and emotional outbursts involving everything from food preparation to medical care.

In the final months, a bad situation became worse because of Granny's dementia. The family didn't have the resources or knowledge to wind their way through the state bureaucracy to qualify Granny for Medicaid placement in an institution. And so, one spring day, the couple dressed Granny in new pajamas, made sure she had no identifying papers, and drove to the local hospital. They got a wheelchair from the waiting room and wheeled Granny into the emergency room. They left her there, sitting in the wheelchair, knowing that someone would eventually notice her and call a nurse. Or maybe Granny would start yelling that she had to use the bathroom.

The hospital was not going to find any information about Granny from her possessions because she didn't have any. And because of her dementia, Granny was no help with the identification questions. The hospital eventually placed her in a local nursing home that accepted Medicaid reimbursement. At last report, there were about 100,000 instances of these "Granny drops" in the United States each year.

There have been major housing changes in the past forty years, some more positive than others. For one thing, there are more nursing homes, although the reluctance to go to a full-care institution has not lessened much. But there are attractive nursing home facilities now, places with in-ground pools and gourmet dining. But many Americans cannot pay the monthly fees in these high-end places, and they have to go to a Medicaid-certified home.

Medicaid institutions are not nearly as attractive. With most current state reimbursement rates, it is difficult to maintain an institution and pay high-caliber staff. Increasing reimbursements to long-term care institutions is never high on any state's priority list. Not incidentally, most nursing home residents do not vote.

However, there has been an explosion in other elderly housing options. Retirement communities are emerging to accommodate the demands of the more affluent baby boomers. The generation that prompted economic ripples in everything from elementary schools to suburban housing is now looking for housing. Individuals who retire in 2024 now have a variety of living options, far more than their grandmothers or even their mothers.

For one thing, Mom can elect to stay where she is, in the home she has lived in for thirty years, because there are home care businesses that will help. If Mom wants to stay in her house, she will be able to hire people to take care of the yard, keep up with the inside household chores, and handle the maintenance problems that come with home ownership. There are also visiting nurse organizations that provide medical care. But staying in her home might not appeal to Mom as much as it once did, especially since many of her neighbors have already moved. Mom will hear or read about all the new retirement villages, many in the southern areas of the country, where sunshine is an attractive natural resource.

As soon as you hit sixty, maybe before, depending on how many mailing lists you are on, you will be showered with brochures depicting happy older people playing golf, making ceramic pots, painting pictures, or sitting around outdoor tables drinking cocktails and laughing with other older people. I always wonder why they are laughing. "Come to a place where the sun always shines! Come enjoy the life you have earned!" so sayeth the colorful brochures.

Why would Mom want to stay in her neighborhood, in a house that needs painting and maybe a new roof? She has lived in that house for thirty years, raised two kids there, divorced her husband who has already headed south, although she isn't sure where, and she managed to maintain the house through all that turmoil. But the neighborhood is not the same. The new guy across the street never cuts his grass, the family next door has four dogs who sometimes do their business on Mom's lawn, and no one in the neighborhood shovels their sidewalks in the winter. She doesn't know any of the newer neighbors. She tried getting acquainted, but younger people don't seem as friendly. If Mom decides to move out of her home, the move will likely be to an "over-fifty-five community," a place where she can be with people "just like her."

Do the professionals writing those brochures ever think about what that phrase "just like you" implies? Exactly who is "just like Mom"? Even though we have largely outgrown that poisonous perspective when it relies on race, religion, or ethnicity, age segregation is apparently acceptable. Where did we get the idea that once you are past a certain age—fifty-five seems to be the common plateau—you have no desire to be anywhere near younger people with children or active single people who have no children but who have loud stereo systems and stay up past midnight doing who knows what?

Anyway, if Mom is looking for a place to retire, to get out of that snowy neighborhood with the dog poop on her lawn, and she wants to live with people her own age, she can now select from a number of housing options. Some elderly enclaves have grown so large that they are, in every sense of the word, self-contained cities. Because of their size and the resident age restrictions, residents never have to watch children play ball in their street or worry that the guy next door might not shovel his sidewalk. Depending on where she moved, Mom might not have to think about snow again.

After a career of watching and talking to individuals who were moving to various retirement settlements and watching people adjusting to their nursing home environments, I was surprised that I was surprised when the time for our own relocation arrived. Bizarre though it might sound, it never occurred to me that our time for such a move would come. I suspect that this "not me, not right now!" perspective is true for many people.

Suddenly—and it does seem to spring up that fast—my wife and I had a line of prescription bottles on the kitchen counter. We wondered where the aches in our various joints came from as we contemplated the day's demanding activities. When did it get so hard to flip the mattress? When did that chainsaw get so heavy? Can we find someone to paint the house?

The signs were there almost every day, pointing to the same troubling conclusion: it was time for us to consider moving out of our beautiful house. I remember listening to older relatives and neighbors as they sat around talking about their age-related problems, saying, "It went so fast."

I remember that I always shook my head—it seems I was shaking my head a lot in my earlier years—finding it hard to believe that anyone's life went that fast. Because when you are young, time often crawls, sometimes at an agonizingly slow pace. Our lives and all the options were in front of us. We couldn't wait to get to our futures because the possibilities seemed endless. Until they weren't.

And so, after talking, debating, and arguing, we decided to think about moving to a retirement community, where we could live that life we had earned. Whatever that meant. As a sociologist, I would have enjoyed sitting on a panel, arguing about the idea of what anyone presumably had "earned," debating how they might have gone about earning it, and if so, exactly what it was that they might have earned.

Anyway, this book describes our traumatic moving process— how the decision was made, the problems involved in moving, the transition to retirement living, what the major adjustments have been, and what our daily life is like now. And what changes has this move made to my perspectives about the world in general and the aging process in particular?

All this personal history is probably more background than you thought you needed or maybe wanted, but believe me, it will help with your understanding of the material. You will be able to understand—to use the popular phrase—where I'm coming from.

I also have a few broader questions that I hope to consider. Is retirement housing a good idea for American society? Would the structure of American communities be improved by making more efforts to keep older citizens in the same neighborhoods, maybe in congregate housing, rather than having them move into gated enclaves, separate from the younger, less experienced citizens who might benefit from such contacts? And what about the effects of the move and the segregation of older citizens? How does moving into the sheltered environments affect them? Or does it affect them?

I'm not sure that this book is going to answer all these questions, but it will try. And if you think it is much too early for you and your spouse to contemplate your own relocation problems, think again!

Because, believe me, it goes so fast . . .

Please note that the following emails have been lightly edited.

Dave:

First of all, I would like to thank you for that birthday card. I would like to, but I can't. Even though your cards are invariably humorous and even more so with your pithy comments, not many individuals can be counted on to make pithy comments, for one thing, because I am not sure what the hell "pithy" means; where was I?

Oh, yes, birthdays, that poisonous index for how another year has passed, you still haven't done shit, and you are even closer to the end of the line when you have to get off, and you wonder where the hell you have been, and you aren't sure if you enjoyed the ride. Is this diatribe making any sense? Was this a metaphor? What is a meta for? (Pause for sustained laughter.)

We are still in the throes of the pandemic here, but I am fast losing my primary excuses for avoiding human contact. Even a few short weeks ago, I could say, "We haven't had our second vaccination yet," or "Are you sure they have their shots?" And lately I have raised the specter of "the delta variant!" But Mery is getting immune (forgive the expression) to my warnings. "I don't give two shits about the delta variant. I want to shop for a new couch."

My newest and surprisingly enjoyable game with Mery involves our living room clock that, despite several trips to the clock repair shop, continues its own interesting mechanical path, which regrettably has nothing to do with the right time. For some reason, the clock always freezes at 3:40, even though I reset it several times a day. When Mer is sitting at her chair pondering her/our next adventure, I will wander by and say, "What time is it?" She glances up at the clock, and for the first few times, she says, "Twenty minutes to four. No, wait, that can't be right. Damn you!" It's amazing how even the small things can give you pleasure during this pandemic.

Outside of COVID, my body continues its steady decline. The middle toe on my right foot, whose nail was ripped out by a podiatrist who reminded me of Bela Lugosi, has healed, albeit with no more toenail. The facial cheek where a cancerous growth was removed in a surgical procedure that resembled scraping the seeds out of an acorn squash has almost healed. My teeth continue to produce problems with depressing regularity. My dentist, by the way, sent me a birthday card lacking in any pithy comments, and it was one of the two cards I received. I think that most people have realized that I do not like birthday celebrations.

On a better news note, the wedding we were going to attend in Illinois has been canceled, apparently because of concern about the delta variant. This family is aware of the transmission possibilities even if Mery is not. This development means we do not have to work our Illinois trip around that often heart-wrenching marital ceremony.

Anyway, Dave, we may be making the trek up there in September rather than October. And I hope we can get together. Maybe Mery will have pictures of our new couch by that time. Don't forget to ask about it. And try your best not to laugh.

Take care of yourself.

Dan

2.

The Big Decision!

The time for our big move arrived! After days that turned into weeks filled with frequent and sometimes emotional discussions—where my line of rebuttal to the growing stack of retirement community brochures was pathetic, along the lines of, "Look at the faces. Some of the people look like paid actors, the same ones who advertise constipation cures. Why would you want to move there?"—we were making the move.

But I'm not sure I used the correct pronoun in that sentence. "She" would have been the more accurate pronoun rather than "we" because Mery had been thinking about this move for a few years. This important fact did not emerge until later in the discussions. And because of her advanced thinking and planning, she had a large, and as it turned out, an insurmountable, lead in her argument portfolio.

Preparation is everything when there is going to be an argument; lawyers, teachers, and politicians know this. It would be nice if the rest of us did. Even though she is not a politician, not in any accepted notion of the term, Mery was ready for the upcoming discussions and I was not.

If the discussions took place in a school room, I would be the student heading into an exam who hadn't had the time or the motivation to study the material because he didn't know there was going to be a test. Or said he didn't know. Anyway, there I was, sitting in the room, looking around, and trying to convey the image of someone who knew what he was going to say. But I didn't.

This decision about moving was not going to be easy even if we started at the same point. How could that decision be anything but difficult when you are talking about not just a change of residence but a major adjustment in lifestyle? This was going to be a major life change, somewhat akin to getting married and setting up your first apartment and realizing, maybe for the first time, how different the two of you were, and what the hell did you think was going to happen when two people occupied the same space?

Can everyone, maybe I should say *anyone*, remember that classic television serial, *Lassie*, where the little boy, I think his name was Jeff, lived with his mom, his beloved gramps, and of course, Lassie? We never found out about the dad. And there was also the local deputy, I think his name was Clay, who constantly prowled around the farm, obviously interested in Mom (Ellen), but I can't remember if that romance went anywhere. Or if there was ever a romance. Ellen seemed primarily interested in Jeff, Gramp's health problems, and making cookies. Ellen never seemed to help out with farm work or cleaning up after Lassie. And she never seemed that involved with poor Clay. And incidentally, who would name their kid Clay? Maybe that name was the underlying problem for Ellen.

Anyway, Gramps finally died, we were never told why, probably overwork, and Ellen decided to sell the farm and move into the city where she thought life would be easier. At least for Ellen. And here's the rub; they couldn't take Lassie. They never explained why, other than "Lassie wouldn't be happy in the city." I think it was because Ellen got tired of dog hair on her furniture. She probably thought she would have more time to make more cookies after the move. And maybe see more of Clay.

It was a very emotional scene when Jeff said goodbye to Lassie, and that, finally, is my point here. When people make a major lifestyle change, the shift can be emotional. This move is not just changing houses; it is changing the way you structure your daily life.

And like Ellen and Jeff, we were shifting into another lifestyle. We can explain the move as justified, even necessary, but it is still going to be hard. Changes mean adjustments, and adjustments take time. I think Ellen would agree, and I know Jeff would. And it would be interesting to find out what Clay thought about it.

Let's go back to our pending relocation. As if we needed more complexities, we had different priorities in mind. I discovered that Mery was worried about her life if I expired suddenly. She began looking at me every morning in an unusually intense fashion. I suppose she had reasons to worry; four of her friends lost their husbands suddenly, and I mean *suddenly*. One guy died sitting in his living room waiting for his wife to finish making snacks. Another one died in his study watching a football game, although this is not a bad way to go if you are a rabid football fan. And he was.

My idea of a good death, if you are comfortable with that idea, involved the father of a friend. The guy was an avid fisherman, and one morning, sitting in his boat with his bait and lunch, his heart gave out when he started his outboard motor. They found his boat later, going in a slow circle on the lake with his body on the bottom of the boat. If you are a serious fisherman, it would be hard to imagine a better death.

Another friend lost her husband to cancer, but no one would pick that unpleasant disease as a good way to go. And when did the term "lost" become so popular when discussing death? If my wife tells me that, "Karen lost her husband," I sometimes respond, "I'm sure she'll find him soon. He might be hiding." My wife does not appreciate humor at a time like that, but in my mind, humor can be an effective way of dealing with difficult situations. If there is a choice between humor and wailing, I'll take humor every time.

Anyway, Mery had the pending death argument, along with her well-thought-out arguments for moving that included the difficulties we had accomplishing routine household chores. Moving a dresser, flipping a mattress, taking an old television set to the dump, assembling a device that your wife ordered in the mail because she thought it was a good deal but turned out to be something you didn't need and didn't work anyway—such tasks, some more important than others, are an integral part of home ownership. And for most of our lives, I had a sense of accomplishment when I finished one of them.

But in increments so small that you don't realize it, the years accumulate, and suddenly, or so it seems, you are waking up more slowly, sometimes with a sore back and pains where you never felt pain before. And it's easier to talk yourself out of doing something around the house. Maybe hold off painting the garage for another year and also decide that the gutters don't need cleaning.

"Are you still enjoying yard work?" Mery asked me one afternoon. I should have been suspicious right away, but I was too tired to be suspicious. I came in the house after a hot morning of weeding, and only homeowners whose house is situated in the mountains can appreciate the unique difficulties of weeding on steep slopes, how tired you get in a relatively short time. Stand up too fast, and you could fall backward. And because you are weeding on your knees and sometimes on your stomach, it is impossible to weed without getting dirty. If it has rained recently, you will also be coated with mud. She caught me in a weak moment because I had been outside after a heavy rain, tired and dirty, but I should've been able to tell she had a topic on mind other than my comfort level.

After a childhood spent in Chicago's South Side neighborhoods, I never got tired of the open areas around our various homes. Nature in North Carolina was a special pleasure—walking, listening to the sounds of distant gunfire, and looking at the mountain landscapes while trying to avoid stepping on a poisonous snake.

After we moved to Asheville, we had a smaller property, but we both loved the mountain view. Sitting on the deck at night, looking at the clear sky, was a treat. But some of the associated chores—the snow shoveling, the gutter cleanings, the window washings, even taking the garbage down the hill once a week—as you get older, can move from tiring to difficult and eventually into potentially dangerous work. You approach the idea of falling differently after you get older. I remember chuckling at the commercials where the individual was lying on the floor and complained, "Help, I've fallen, and I can't get up!" The laments weren't so funny anymore.

When we lived in Michigan's Upper Peninsula, I had a chore that had to be done two or three times each year. Our house was surrounded by pine trees, and those picturesque trees shed their needles with depressing regularity. Those needles landed on our house and garage roofs. Pine needles are acidic and, if left on asphalt roofs, will eat away at shingles. I had a feeling that the pine needles were eating our shingles. Obviously, that was an idiotic perspective. On the other hand, I could post that statement on Facebook, and who knows? My bizarre perspective might be cited in a congressional hearing about the advantages of clear-cutting national forests because of the harm caused by hungry pine needles.

Anyway, several times a year, I would grab my leaf blower, climb onto the roofs, and blow the needles off. Once they were on the ground, I gave them no further thought. I was not one of those people who raked pine needles and hauled them into the forest. If the needles wanted to go to the forest, let them walk. None of the neighbors ever commented on the amount of pine needles accumulating in our yard. That was a little surprising because the needles got thick enough to qualify as a carpet. But that's one of the things I liked about Michigan's Upper Peninsula. Very few people were devoted to their lawns, and they cared even less about yours.

In Michigan, we lived in what you could call a hillside ranch, and the south roof was two stories above the ground. When I operated the leaf blower and got close to the edge of the roof to move all the hungry pine needles, that was always an uncomfortable feeling. You are standing at the edge of the roof and wonder what it would be like to tumble down two stories into the cold lake waters. I would never have lasted with a job in high-rise construction.

All these memories meant that we had a compelling list of reasons to relocate to more comfortable quarters. Our moving discussions generated a lot of advice from well-meaning friends. "Well, you should hire someone to do the work!" was common advice when complaining about the exertions of home maintenance. But as many homeowners will attest, getting help is not easy—unless you have a large and available family group.

It is unfair to criticize a family member because they aren't available to mow their mother's lawn. Children have their own families and maintenance problems to handle. Assuming you can't count on family members for assistance in chores like cleaning the pine needles off a roof, you have to find someone to do the job. That may not be possible, even if you are willing to pay.

Here is an interesting, and maybe not that unusual, story about the problems that can spring up with home maintenance. One summer, we were in Michigan but had to return two weeks early; our neighbor called to tell us that the local rains had been torrential and our neighborhood had a major power failure. A power failure meant that our crawl space sump pumps might not be working, and that situation spelled trouble. We had to head home.

Sure enough, when we got back to Illinois and lifted the trap door to the crawl space, there were four feet of water sitting down there. Our furnace and well water holding tanks were in that water, so we had to do something. Or, preferably, hire someone to do something because my back was having spasms just thinking about what work might be necessary!

Not incidentally, if any of you are looking for a home, I suggest you stay away from any dwelling built on a crawl space. These spaces, usually three or four feet deep, are fine if nothing important is down there. But if the builder put appliances there, after a few years, when your legs get stiffer, and your back gets tender, you will curse his memory and sully his reputation to anyone who will listen. But no one will. I contacted a few furnace repair places, and each one said the same thing, in slightly different ways. "We're not going down there for any repairs, not until you get the water out."

After several fruitless calls, I put on a bathing suit and dove into—actually, I slipped into—the incredibly cold water and swam the length of the house to the sump pump. I freed up the sump pump that was blocked by debris, and water started flowing from the pump into our saturated backyard. That presented different problems, but I won't discuss them now.

After the water was gone, it took two days for the furnace guy to come to the house. And it was no surprise when he told us that we needed a new furnace. The poor guy didn't want to go into the crawl space to install one even though it was relatively dry by then, and I don't fault him. Installing a furnace and removing the old one is difficult enough. But if you have to do the work on your knees, the job becomes torturous. He did the job, but not graciously. Repair people do not like crawl spaces. Keep this in mind when you are considering changing homes or building one. If you, or anyone else, has repair work to perform in your crawl space, you are not going to like it! And it will get worse as the years go by.

It was also no surprise that our insurance did not cover the furnace replacement. "Your policy does not cover sump pump failure," the agent said. I tried to explain, without screaming, that it was the rain that caused the flooding and the sump failure. And, as usual with insurance claims, I had to go over his head with my appeal. Insurance agents, as many Americans know, are trained to sell, not to settle claims. And appeals to insurance companies seldom go anywhere other than to the "coverage appeal" desks that are staffed with trained individuals, all of whom have "claim denied!" stamps on their desks. In my mind, an accurate motto for insurance companies would be, "We sell, but we do not cover."

Anyway, this sad story is just one negative example for those people who insist you can "just find someone to do the work." Of course, finding someone is only the first step in what could be a long process. You also have to consider whether you can afford the work.

Major household repairs are rarely part of any family's monthly budget. You may set aside money for furnace filters but not for replacing or repairing the furnace. Budgeting for basic maintenance work or appliance replacements is often a strain and often postponed. So, when you need the money, it may not be there, and you start thinking about a homeowner loan.

Finally, you want to be confident that the work satisfies you, that your immediate problem has been solved, and that the solution did not make it worse. Homeowners today have the advantage of online services that "rate" repairmen, and that service is not a bad place to start your search for help. The rating services are better than nothing. But sometimes not that much better. The contractors pay a fee to these presumably objective referring agencies, so there is an apparent conflict of interest. You could end up with a plumbing contractor, as we did, a man who spent three months doing nothing other than explaining to us why he hadn't done anything.

Like most homeowners, we rely on "word-of-mouth" recommendations rather than online agencies.

I remember our neighbor in Hampshire, Illinois, telling us, "Remember, no matter where you go, there you are!" He said that a lot.

Mery had a lengthy list that argued against us remaining in our house, and repair problems were high on that list. She argued that the universe told us to "get the hell out of there while you still can." She introduced this interesting notion of "the universe" whenever it helped her argument. I never rebutted it because I had no idea who or what "the universe" was and where its arguments might be posted.

But there were also the more positive "pull factors" operating during the difficult decision process. One example would be a close childhood friend living where you plan on going. She assures you that "you are going to love it here." We didn't have anyone telling us that, but one factor pulling us toward a retirement community instead of renting an apartment was the absence of outdoor and indoor maintenance. Retirement communities tell prospective buyers that there is "nothing to think about except enjoying yourselves."

And we thought it might be nice to have recreational facilities, like a swimming pool and hiking trails. We could plan trips without worrying about a furnace failure. It is fascinating how people can gush about certain things when they are looking for new housing, and after they get everything arranged in their new places, they never use the things they gushed over just a few weeks earlier.

The personable retirement community sales associates reminded me of the salespeople in commercials who point out beautiful new cars with features you will never use. Salespeople are masters at gushing and getting you to gush along with them. They gush as they explain the various features their community provides to its residents. "I can just see you on our hiking trails."

We looked at one retirement community, and among other accouterments, it had a spacious hot tub for resident use. Hot tubs always look great in a brochure. You see clips of attractive people sipping cocktails, smiling, and reclining in the community hot tub, with bubbles popping everywhere. A happy picture, and it is easy to picture yourself there with one of those iced cocktails. But if I thought about it, I could not conjure up many people I would want sitting by me in a hot tub. I doubt whether many people would enjoy bathing with other individuals.

In one of our weaker moments—and we had weak moments more often when we were younger—we installed one of those hot water containers outside our house. We did most of the work, and now that I think back, we did all of it. The only thing the retail store did was sell us the tub, with a cover that cost extra, and deliver the accursed thing. I thought I saw a sinister smile on the delivery guy's face when he left, but it might have been my imagination.

There is a surprising amount of electrical prep work for outdoor hot water heaters. And you also have to consider the site preparation.

My father-in-law was an electrician (not licensed, but he worked on his home wires a lot). I think he liked the designation, so he never corrected us. Anyway, he helped with the hookup. I never guessed the size of the electrical coil that ran from the tub to the house. I expected to use a regular extension cord, maybe a little thicker, but we had to run a new cord with the thickness of a garden hose.

It was only after we spent some time soaking in the tub that we read a magazine article describing hot tubs as "caldrons of infections." This was not the description we wanted to read. The critical piece—I think it had a title like, "Stay away from hot tubs!"—described the containers as life-sized petri dishes filled with viruses that don't have names yet. Why is it that we never encounter critical articles until after we purchase an item?

When I thought about it, that petri dish metaphor made sense. All sorts of people jumped into our hot tub because it was outside. You want to be a nice neighbor. "Bill, you're all sweaty from shoveling out your horse barn. Why don't you hop into our hot tub and relax?"

It turns out that Bill had been working in his barn for several days and hadn't had time for baths, so whatever germs and toxins he accumulated in the barn would now be reproducing in our hot tub. After I thought about it—once I get negative thoughts, they come in a stream—it would not have surprised me if neighbors or delivery workers took a quick soak if we were not home to object. But we would probably have encouraged them anyway because the tub was just sitting there, no one was using it, and what could be the harm?

Installing that hot tub turned out to be one of the silliest things we ever did. And that is saying a lot! For several weeks, two or three in the spring and maybe two weeks in the fall, taking off our clothes and slipping into the hot tub was a great experience. But doing it during the harsh Midwestern winter? That experience was *extremely* painful.

I admit that it was nice, relaxing by ourselves in a hundred-degree hot tub while snow was falling. Staring at the stars, feeling the bubbles swirling around all the areas of your body. But eventually, you have to get out of the tub and put the cover back on before you go into the warm house. Have you ever been soaking wet on a ten-degree, windy evening and had to spend four or five minutes, maybe more, fastening the cover on your hot tub? And you would still be naked if you didn't have a robe, and I did not have a robe.

After one of those experiences, I didn't feel warm for the rest of the night. Sometimes into the next day. During the winter months, I vowed not to go into that tub again until spring, a promise that I never kept. And I don't want to talk about the effect the hot tub had on our electric bills.

Enough about hot tubs! Another important consideration when moving involves the disposal issue, a problem or situation often described as "downsizing." No matter what they call it, you will have a lot of stuff to get rid of. When moving into smaller quarters, one of your immediate concerns is disposing of the stuff that you've accumulated over the years. And you might be surprised that few of your family or friends will be interested in any of your stuff.

By "stuff," I mean items you bought or inherited and then retained but never used. And you don't intend to take the stuff with you because you can't because there is no room. When you think about the stuff you have sitting around the house and garage, some in original boxes, you will reach the same surprising conclusion I did, that you use a few household items all the time and never use the rest. I will cite one sad example: the knife set we have had in our kitchen since the Carter years. There must be ten or twelve knives embedded in the attractive wood stand, and I have yet to pull any of them out. I have the knives I use all the time in the kitchen drawer.

I'm not sure why we even bought that knife stand. I admit that it looks good, standing tall on the counter, all the knives waiting to be called into service. Most cooks on television shows seem to be pulling knives from their stands. But we never have. You think it would be easy to dispose of that knife holder, but it wasn't. "We may need that sometime," was Mery's explanation.

Everyone should walk through a county fair because it provides insight into how many people are spending their time making things no one needs. But when these talented artisans bring their wares to the local fairground booths, their items sell like hotcakes. I presume, at one time, hotcakes sold very well. But in searching my memory, I'm not sure I have ever even seen a hotcake.

Anyway, at one of those fairgrounds, we bought a large birch birdhouse we didn't need and I didn't want. It came with a porch that looked neat at a fairground booth, although you might have wondered what kind of bird would be looking for a place with a porch. But you learn quickly that fairground birdhouses are not meant for the birds. You bring the item home, and in a short time, maybe even that evening, you wonder what the hell you were thinking.

I was not going to put it in the yard, so we took it to the garage, and there it sat for several years. We would have taken it to the basement if we had one. But now we are selling the house, and the realtor shakes her head at the accumulated clutter and advises us to get rid of all the "stuff" before she takes any pictures to feature on the internet.

Imagine what is going to happen, the additional work for you, when realtors begin showing film clips of your home. I'm guessing it won't be long before they hire actors, B or even C level actors, to do various chores as they film your house and its surroundings. I can see it now; the film crews surprise the homeowner as they come into the house.

Maybe there will be a guy in the kitchen, who looks like Mark Hamill, and he'll be making a batch of chili, smiling as he slices and dices the various ingredients, selecting several knives from the attractive wooden stand on the kitchen counter to chop the fresh ingredients waiting on the sparkling clean counter. I've made a lot of chili in my time, and I have never smiled as I cut the ingredients. When I work on onions and jalapeno peppers, I'm usually in tears. And the counter looks more like an urban alley.

But it's not a bad idea, really, watching Mark Hamill, who I don't believe has done much acting since *Star Wars*, working in the kitchen and telling the camera, "This kitchen is large enough for me to make my signature chili without getting in my wife's way. Look over there, and you'll see her fixing the dishwasher. She is one amazing woman!" The camera then turns slowly to someone who looks a little like Angelina Jolie, and the actress smiles as she tightens a bolt. As though any of us are going to believe that this woman just fixed a dishwasher, the nearest thing to an unfixable appliance.

Once we started on the clutter, it amazed both of us, mostly me, how much stuff we had. We considered ourselves to be minimalists—well, one of us is. We never needed a lot of stuff, but that didn't stop one of us from buying a birdhouse with a porch, among other things. There was no way to deny it—all the accumulated stuff was there, staring at us, some in boxes, some in plastic bags, stuff like two matching bowling balls that may have been Christmas gifts from someone who thought we liked to bowl, but we didn't. Mery is fond of bringing out a bowling trophy she won in high school, and this may have prompted that gift. By the way, this high school trophy was also in our garage. We had an accordion in the garage that I hadn't played since I was a kid and hated even then, three broken dining room chairs from a set long gone, but you never know, and, well, you get the idea.

The potentially divorce-inducing problem was deciding what to get rid of and what to keep. I think it is fair to say, and I hope it will not be interpreted as sexism, that males are quicker to dispose of stuff than females are. Women seem to be more emotionally involved and can attach significance to some strange items. "Oh, that was little Karen's first crib. We can't give that away."

You want to scream. I did scream once or twice. For one thing, we didn't have a little Karen. But we did have "Mom's china." Mom's china (MC) is a set of unattractive dishes given to my wife by her mother. I don't think it is important where her mom got that china. Maybe at a gas station, when gas stations used to promote their products and services with small gifts like glasses or coffee cups.

The dishes were housed in heavy cardboard boxes that I have carried from house to house over the years. I think we did use MC three times in thirty years. But I could be wrong about this. You don't have to be a whiz at long division to see that we used MC every ten or fifteen years. Not worth the trouble by any reasonable measure. Definitely not by mine.

Anyway, the coffee cups were too small to satisfy anyone's coffee thirst; they could be described as "demitasse cups." And the dinner plates were nowhere near large enough for a major dinner. If your meal included items that needed space, let's say spaghetti and meatballs with garlic bread, your dinner guests would be looking around for where to put their salad and dinner rolls.

When we used MC, we could count on considerable food residue—various sauces and crumbs on the table after the guests left, maybe still hungry because the plates were not large enough to hold a sufficient amount of food. And if that wasn't enough, although in my mind it was, you couldn't put the damn dishes in the dishwasher. They were "too delicate."

My role model in household disposal cases involves my friend, Dave, the executor of his aunt's estate. His aunt was a successful travel agent who accumulated treasures from all over the world. Her impressive background and varied experiences didn't faze Dave. He went into her condo like the vandals entering Rome. If it was the vandals.

Dave kept a few items and turned the rest of the treasures over to the local consignment shop with instructions to donate anything they could not sell. In three hours, that fossil-rich apartment was picked clean. Aunt Hildy's valuable stuff disappeared into Florida's stream of secondhand consumer goods. Dave was back home in two days; mission accomplished.

On my list of practical problems stemming from a downsizing move to a retirement community, I would place item disposal near the top. Because you are not going to have room for everything.

Retirement living is, almost by definition, going to involve considerable downsizing, and you must come to terms with that. If you need a ballpark figure, and who doesn't, count on getting rid of at least half of what you currently have on your shelves and in your garage. Maybe more, depending on how big a house you have and, of course, the size of your new retirement home.

Maybe you could call Dave. Or someone like him, if you know such a person, because I don't think Dave likes doing that kind of thing. And I know he doesn't like calls. But it is far easier to get rid of something if you have no emotional attachment to the item. And that's what you are going to need, the absence of emotional attachment to items such as Mom's china. Looking at an item and deciding to get rid of it is difficult, made even tougher when there is arguing about what is valuable.

But now there are the storage sheds. I remember when storage facilities started popping up in urban and suburban landscapes. And "popping up" is the right description. A vacant lot on Friday could, by Monday morning, be a new storage facility with chain link fencing and a large billboard telling passing motorists, "Climate-controlled units are now available!"

I remember thinking at the time, *What nonsense! Who is going to rent more closet space?* The answer is, a lot of people; we had to get on waiting lists at a few facilities. And the rents are more than we paid for our first apartment. I count this as another missed investment opportunity. I remember saying the same thing when Starbucks first started. "Who is going to pay that kind of money for a cup of coffee?"

It would be an interesting study to look at the correlation between the fairly recent emergence of retirement communities and the growth of storage facilities. Every time we talk to other residents and ask what they did with the stuff from their 4,000-square-foot homes, they reply, "Oh, we rented a storage shed. We got a climate-controlled one right down the street." Renting one of those storage facilities might be another case of kicking the can down the road, but moving is difficult enough. It might be best for everyone if they postpone taking their birdhouses to a resale shop until the emotional climate is more settled. If it ever does get settled.

Another difficult issue for us involved dogs. We have had dogs, golden retrievers, two at a time, for thirty years, and we loved spending time with every one of them. But as every dog person knows, having those affectionate companions in your home comes with a hefty emotional price. You are eventually going to be faced with putting your dog down.

We had to do that painful chore six times. It never got any easier, and the process of putting the last two down was so difficult that we agreed to postpone discussions about adopting more dogs until our housing plans were finalized. Another of our few items of total agreement was that an apartment was no place for a golden retriever. If we ended up in an apartment, as we did, then we would not be looking for another dog.

And so, over the span of a few months, we discussed the pushes and pulls, the pluses and the minuses, the good and the bad, and the yings and the yangs. We came up with the same answer every time, that moving out of our house made sense. It may have made sense, but I still wasn't ready. I'm not sure I ever would have been under normal circumstances, whatever those are, but there was one final push, the exceptionally hot real estate market during 2022. It was as if the universe was saying, "Hey, how much encouragement do you need?"

Unfortunately, I have never been an advocate of listening to the universe. As I mentioned earlier, I don't even know what people have in mind when they use that term. I decided that it was just a catchall term, something to cut off further discussion. And it usually works. Some of our previous home sales took a long time. It's hard to understand why a home that you regarded as ideal, that has served you well for years, prompts potential buyers to walk through the house with scowls and say, "Why did they put a patio door there?" Or "Why would anyone paint one bedroom wall red?"

I want to answer that last question because readers might wonder the same thing. But my wife saw the color contrast in a magazine and thought it looked good. We tried it, and it did look good. Actually, I thought it looked great, but I have never been known for decorating. The one red wall really accented the rest of the room, although I have no idea what that means.

Our Michigan place, a fairly large house on a lake across from a national forest and one of our favorite places to live, took five years to sell. Even the local realtors couldn't understand it. That frustrating experience can sour you about the speed of home selling, so we were understandably anxious to take advantage of the hot Asheville home market. You never know how long a hot market will last.

One agent told us that the current market was so crazy that we could put curtains on our backyard storage shed, list it as a tiny house, price it "as is" for fifty thousand dollars, and we might receive four offers the first week. That statement sounded like gushing on the order of "languishing in your comfortable hot tub." But we decided to let the real estate market be the final deciding factor in our potential relocation. I wouldn't have been disappointed had our house not sold and we had to stay for a few more years. But the house sold on the first day. And it was, to quote *The Godfather*, an offer we couldn't refuse.

And so, like it or not, we were going to move, and we were going to have to get rid of a lot of stuff. But we still had to decide where we were going! And naturally, the universe was no help with this next decision. We were on our own.

Dave:

This is another sad moving story. I should probably have written "a sad story about moving," lest you think I am slipping into redundancy when I write. At least it is sad if you have any feelings left in your cynical mind.

And I will be the first to admit it; well, maybe not the first, but not the last either. Anyway, we can agree that Americans have been spoiled, but life when there is an active quarantine in the country is not easy. Among other things, you find yourself doing jobs around the house more to stay busy than because of any pressing need. But in this case, because we are moving, there is a pressing need for tasks that you would otherwise ignore.

By the way, Dave, have you ever thought about the origin or meaning of a "pressing task"? For example, when you are reading about the world's most pressing issues, do you know what they refer to? Do such critical thoughts ever enter your cluttered mind?

Anyway, Mery and I have not yet killed one another, but we are getting closer. This morning, as part of our early morning "What unnecessary moving task should we undertake today?" process, we cleaned the garage. This cleaning apparently is a necessary step in getting ready to sell the house, and it did not go well. I am more convinced than ever that there is no good reason for a man and a woman to jointly clean a garage. The two sexes are just not psychologically equipped to work together on such tasks.

A garage is a place to store things that do not belong in the house and can't be left outside. This would include items like lawn mowers, the ones currently working and those you plan to repair, chain saws, old hoses you haven't patched yet, and rusty gas cans. You don't expect, at least I don't, such items to look neat. They are in your garage, for god's sake.

Unfortunately, the male/female perspectives on garages are about as far apart as you can get. Here are a few typical confrontations from our morning's work:

"Where does this tool go?" she asked, holding up needle-nosed pliers.

Now, like most guys, I put tools where I can reach them. Or where I set them after I'm finished with a job. This is why I constructed a large work bench in the garage. But Mery thought it made more sense to arrange the tools alphabetically and to put them away, whatever that means. Thus, all three of my needle-nosed pliers belong in the drawer with my other pliers (labeled P), the drawer located below my drill bits (D), but above my screwdrivers (S).

Have you ever tried arranging a paint shelf by color? Paint stores may do this, and I suppose it is helpful—I never thought about it—but garage shelves? We now have our paint cans of whites in the back, reds at the front, and green in the middle, somewhat like a rainbow I suppose. I am amazed at how many half-full cans of paint I have accumulated over the years. I have a great paint can story, but I don't think I will take the time now to relate it, mostly because I don't think you give a shit about such unusual personal events.

But would any guy ever, even in his more desperate moments, think about running a vacuum cleaner over the garage floor? But we did it that morning. Or Mery did it. "I don't know how you can work here with all the dust." She assumed I felt some guilt about the dirt and sawdust on the floor. I did not.

"And why don't you paint that pegboard on the wall;

that brown is such a drab color. And while you're at it, put those hooks in a neat row instead of scattered all over."

Well, the garage is organized now, but I have no idea where the hell anything is. Tomorrow, we are tackling the bathroom medicine cabinets "to get all that stuff organized according to affliction. We'll put all the salves underneath on a separate shelf."

For the historical record, in case anyone is keeping track of such things, I understand the need to straighten out things in our house in preparation for the upcoming house listing, a time when you realize that you really no longer own the place. Ownership has passed to the real estate people. This demeaning sales process can't end soon enough for me. The virus might not kill me, but the future prospect of cleaning out the closets and organizing my clothes by season and color—that task may be my undoing.

And Dave, if you have not started your own garage cleaning, please know that you are in my thoughts and prayers. On the other hand, you might have more pressing issues to worry about.

Dan

3.

Where Are We Going?

If you haven't moved to a retirement community before, then believe me when I tell you this is different than any other move. For one thing, it is likely going to be your last major housing change. Well, the next to last, so you want to be especially cautious.

This time, our decision was not going to be about styles—ranch or two-story—and do we want a full basement? Or a crawl space? (No chance of that!) What about a fenced-in yard? It is interesting that there aren't many fenced yards in retirement communities. At least we didn't find any, and I think that would be yet another interesting research project.

When I was teaching and had a research inspiration but no time or inclination to pursue it, I would give graduate students the topic. They were always hungry for research projects, and giving them research ideas made us all happy. Especially me—I got my questions answered without exertion.

About moving, we had to think about more than the design of the house; we were selecting a community and its lifestyle. We had to take time to pick what would make us the most comfortable, and we knew it wasn't going to be easy. Part of my unease was that I wasn't sure where and what made me most comfortable; once again, Mery had a head start. She knew what she wanted and guided me in that direction with the finesse of a high school guidance counselor.

Much better, actually, because my high school guidance counselor provided virtually no counseling and a similar amount of guidance. Mery didn't have to worry about having big shoes to fill.

First, we considered geography, and that characteristic was on both our lists. What I heard a lot—in fact, I had made the statement myself—was, after retirement, *I'm moving to a place where I don't see snow, and I won't feel cold when I step outside.* I never loved shoveling the white stuff, although I admit I enjoyed riding my tractor that came with a snow blower attachment. In Illinois, I often drove it to the neighbor's house to do his driveway. Part of that was to help him, but it was also great to stay on that machine with the powerful blower.

Driving the tractor into the snowbanks and watching the snow being thrown into the air made the hours required to install that snowblower almost worth it. The operators of the county highway plows must feel like they are driving tanks in a battle zone. Driving a snowplow puts you in command of the snowstorm. A good feeling!

Anyway, the large number of retirement communities springing up in places like Arizona and Florida testify to the popularity of the anti-snow sentiment. But we also had to think about leaving friends and families, although some of them were migrating as well. It was as though our campsite was breaking up, and all the campers headed in different directions—all bound for what they presumed to be better lives. It is a sad realization that the community you were so comfortable in is breaking up, and there isn't much you can do about it. You can't convince people to stay when they think it is time for them to leave.

And were we ready for that personal loss? Long-distance friendships are harder to maintain; we knew that. When people move, there are always sincere promises to "keep in touch" and "get together regularly." The promises are seldom kept, not because the intentions aren't good, but because the logistics are not. It is difficult to drive 600 miles to see an old friend when you used to meet at a local restaurant every Thursday for dinner or stop at their house for coffee. But at least we didn't have to worry about moving away from the kids because there were no kids to move away from.

We decided to focus the search on North Carolina. We were already there, we lived there part-time for ten years, and we liked it. The state has a moderate climate and a variety of housing options. Driving around the state, you get the feeling that retirement housing is one of North Carolina's major industries, along with craft beer. I don't believe these two things are connected, but it's another interesting research project. Good beer is a drawing card for some people. Great coffee would draw me, but not great beer.

We started looking and leaving our names on the guest registers—in retrospect, this was not a good idea; our mailbox was regularly packed with brochures and personal letters, all telling us that this particular development was geared to providing us "the lives we have earned."

How would they know this information? Have they been keeping a file? What happens to the people stopping by who haven't earned that lifestyle? Are they turned away? Are they offered different homes? And none of these places told us what our earned lifestyle was. Did the lifestyles always involve sitting in hot tubs and playing golf?

We looked at a few high-rise buildings close to the Asheville downtown area. The locations were ideal, but the buildings, advertised as ideal senior living, provided few support services. Sometimes none. We lived in downtown Asheville for a few months and loved it, but it did not fit Mery's as yet undeclared requirements. So, only one of us looked closely at the downtown apartment option.

We also had to consider finances. Did we want to select a place with a monthly rental fee that was obviously going to go up over the years, or opt to buy a place and consume a good portion of our retirement savings but not have to worry about rent increases?

It's not important, but I have never liked the term "nest egg." I understand what the term implies; I just never thought it did the job. I was more comfortable with the standard term "retirement savings."

There was a fairly new financial option out there in retirement land. Many retirement communities now have sizable entrance fees that give the buyer the right to rent their home or apartment for life, or for as long as they can maintain the unit and pay the rent. The hardest thing to wrap our heads around was that you were not purchasing anything except the right to live in the community.

The first time we encountered that financial arrangement, we dismissed it as a version of time-share for retirees. But as we looked at a variety of settings, including some in Illinois, we realized that the arrangement was more common than we thought. This financial arrangement obviously would not suit every retiree's needs. Or their finances. It apparently serves the needs of the people who finance these retirement communities.

We looked at several communities that offered different financial commitments, some with townhouses, others with individual homes, and usually with fifty to a hundred homes, sometimes more. Most had amenities such as a pool, clubhouse, and the occasional hot tub. All the retirement communities required applicants to be at or above the age of fifty-five. I have been somewhat cynical for most of my life, so I assumed that if a couple, both age forty-six, put cash down on a unit, no one was going to challenge the purchase. Oscar Wilde put this perspective beautifully: "When I was young I thought that money was the most important thing in life; now that I am old, I know that it is!"

Retirement communities are usually well-defined areas, sometimes with fencing, and some have what I—I'm kidding, of course—describe as "guard towers" at entrances. Builders apparently believe that older people are obsessed with personal safety, and their potential customers would be drawn to a guarded entry. No one gets in who doesn't belong! Intruders will be shot! No, we never encountered a sign like that. But I wonder if some potential residents would be attracted to that sign.

I have the feeling that builders of these retirement communities look at the older segment of society in the same way hungry wolves look at a flock of wild turkeys. I suppose that the proper term is a "rafter of turkeys." I wonder if older English teachers ever outgrow their need to correct someone's grammar. Anyway, older Americans obviously represent an appealing, lucrative, and growing market.

I admit our search was not exhaustive because I have a low tolerance for shopping. Shopping for anything, especially homes, exhausts me. Psychologically, not physically. I wish it weren't this way, but after five or ten stops, the places and items start to look alike. I couldn't remember who had the largest hot tub and which ones had walking trails. I developed an intolerance for the well-dressed salespeople telling us, "We would love to have you as residents." Their statements sounded like all the car salesmen I have encountered over the years. "What do I have to do to put you in this car today, Dan?"

After finishing one of those excessively long "Did you look at the size of our community hot tub? Can't you picture yourself sitting in there?" visits, Mery often wondered if the sales rep would be disappointed if we moved elsewhere. In Mery's words, "She seemed so intent on our moving there. Maybe we should write to her and explain why we decided against their establishment." Mery was surprised when I didn't agree, and I was surprised at her surprise.

"I doubt the lady remembered our names ten minutes after we left," I assured my wife, but I don't think I convinced her. She probably sent apologetic emails to every sales rep we met.

We finally made our selection. And once again, the pronoun is misleading. Mery always planned on picking a full-care location, a community where she could continue to live after I died and not have to worry about selling a home and moving again, this time without me in the background making useless suggestions and wondering when we could have dinner. The dying idea, my dying, apparently played a major part in our/her decision. Not that we hadn't discussed it before. Death discussions tend to emerge as you get older. Your relatives start dropping off the Christmas card list, and your friends start reporting the presence of terminal illnesses. Such inevitable and always sad events take a toll on your thinking.

Weeding names out of our phone directory has turned into a yearly holiday procedure. Mery goes through her directory and crosses off the names of those people who have gone to their rewards. As far as I am concerned, although I'm not sure how far that is, that sobering process of directory weeding can be regarded as the final stage for someone's existence on the planet. Their names are wiped from personal directories all across the country, and this finishes the dying process.

Dying is one of the last things we are going to do. No, strike that! It is absolutely the last thing we are going to do, and I think it is fair to say that no matter what our education, income level, political persuasion, or religious affiliation, we want to do it well. You don't want your friends and relatives thinking about your death, "It must have been terrible for him. And for poor Mery." What you might say if you knew that your friend had been eaten by a shark when he was sitting in his paddle boat enjoying the sunshine.

Unfortunately, very few of us get to choose the manner and timing of our demise. If I had any choice in the matter, I would opt for Spencer Tracy's character in *The Last Hurrah*, a great movie based on the book by Edwin O'Connor. If you haven't seen it or read it, put it on your list. If you have a list.

Anyway, watch for that final scene when there is a crowd around the mayor's bed. Everyone assumes the mayor has already slipped away, and this guy who never liked the mayor is gloating about the mayor's demise. This particular actor seems to be the bad guy in every movie. He says to the other individuals standing around the bed that if there's one thing we can all be sure of, there's no doubt the mayor would do it very differently if he could do it all over again.

Spencer (the mayor) opens his eyes, looks at the asshole, and says, "Like hell I would!" Then he dies, this time for good. Great scene, and more importantly, what a great way to die! Even his grieving relatives had to smile. Movie deaths can be pretty attractive, or as attractive as a death can be.

Another good death also came from a movie. I can't recall the title or even who starred in it. Ward Bond could have been in it. That guy must have been in a hundred movies, and I think I have seen at least ten of them. Anyway, the actors were in a small boat drifting in a vast ocean, and the lead character knew it made sense for him to sacrifice himself because it would help the other people on the boat. Early one morning, he pushed himself off the boat and drifted away.

You wonder how everyone would have been asleep because it wasn't a hotel where all the lights were turned off, and it was time for everyone to sleep. Anyway, when the rest of the group got up—maybe they wished they smelled coffee perking, but of course, that was impossible—they realized what their friend did during the night; they collectively gasped and then went about the business of surviving, something that would now be easier because there was one less person to ask for a drink of the scarce water. Another good movie death! But that was because we didn't have to watch the guy drown.

George Burns had a great line that guided his nightclub performances. "Always leave them wanting more!" He was talking about being on the stage, but he could just as easily be referring to our presence on the planet. Very few of us like the prospect of being confined to a bed or sitting in a chair all day, complaining about ailments, and watching daytime television. But things are different now. Medical technology can keep us watching television far beyond our capacity to derive any benefit from it. If there is any benefit from daytime television.

It is getting harder and harder to have a good death because your doctor and the hospital may not let you. When my father was in the hospital, I showed up one morning and discovered he was connected to a ventilator. They were also giving him Haldol, a powerful tranquilizer, because according to the nurse, "he was visibly upset."

Who wouldn't be upset? Besides, it never took much to upset my father. I asked the nurse to disconnect the ventilator and stop giving him Haldol. But my request was not like saying to a restaurant server, "No, I ordered the pork chop without gravy." This was a medical request I was making, and someone had to authorize the major change.

After several discussions with various levels of hospital authority, I said that if they did not respect my wishes, I would have my father transferred to another facility and sue the hospital for malpractice. They made the changes I requested, and my father died the day after, so no further arguing was necessary. Dying can be as hard a process as living, sometimes harder!

Back to our housing decision, I understood what Mery had in mind with her housing selections. She had a few unpleasant hospital experiences with her family, vivid memories of her relatives in various states of consciousness, drifting in and out of awareness, with tubes and wires plugged into their already riddled bodies. I wanted to see myself departing life like Spencer Tracey, shaking my fist at the injustices and the bad people.

Getting back to that moving decision, or decision about moving, we decided on a retirement complex in Asheville, one with a variety of housing options and provision for full nursing care should either of us eventually need it. We felt comfortable with the prospect that once we moved to this place, we would not have to move again. Until, of course, that final move. We have also settled that difficult question, but that is a separate topic.

A major element in moving is the physical part, the act of moving. You have to get your stuff from point A to point B. Or for us, from point A to point B and then finally to point C. As we age, many of us choose to delegate this chore to professionals. This was going to be the first time we were relying on professionals to handle our household move, although we—and I should say, "I"—have a lot of experience with the relocation process.

In our early years, Mery would farm me out to whoever needed help. "Dan loves to help people move," she would say, and to this day, I don't know where she got that ridiculous idea. No matter who was involved, I hated that time-consuming chore from the time of the initial packing until the time I stacked the last box. I especially hated picking up heavy furniture and moving it through narrow doorways, bruising my fingers in the process. I hated picking up dressers with the drawers still inside, knowing it would be unnecessarily heavy. I hated when people would say, "Of course we're taking our new refrigerator."

I didn't like the process when it was our furniture, but I really hated the process when it involved other people's. Sometimes, I comforted myself by thinking, *At least I'll receive a good meal at the end*; that positive event rarely happened. When people move, most of their items involving meal preparation are packed. They never have a grill ready to pop steaks onto because the grill is packed, or it was sold with the house. If you get any food, it's likely fish filets from McDonald's or food from some other fast-food establishment. A word of advice: if you are offered a fish filet that has been sitting on someone's kitchen counter for a few hours, take a pass! You will be far better off if you nibble on some crackers.

Mery and I have moved a lot, both when we were kids and after we got married. When you add it up, as we have done several times because we seem to enjoy that kind of thing, we have been involved in about forty moves. But our perspectives about all this moving are slightly different. Let me rephrase that; they are totally different.

Mery thinks that moving is exciting, a chance to refresh your pattern of living, wipe the board of uncomfortable furniture arrangements, and start fresh. Add some new furniture. She loves to remove everything from a closet and reorganize everything in a new and presumably more efficient arrangement.

She seems fascinated by the opportunity to wipe every surface clean before stacking anything on it or in it. When contemplating a move, she gets the same look in her eyes as I imagine Davy Crockett got in his when his friend said, "We should head west, Davy. What about Texas? We could be comfortable there."

I admit that Mery is very organized about moving. She packs boxes in categories, tapes the boxes with furniture tape, and labels each one with her precise printing. When I pack, I grab whatever is handy and throw it into any available container. My stated mission is to get everything packed and ready to load, and "categories" are the furthest thing from my mind. It is easy to understand why moving is often at or near the top of marital frustration lists.

When we unpacked, if it was a box I loaded, we never had any idea of what was going to be inside. Kind of fun! The box could easily contain two sweaters, some printer ink, a photo album, and maybe two or three cans of green beans. If we tear open one of Mery's containers, labeled "kitchen," then you can be sure that everything in that box will go on one of the clean kitchen shelves. Or in the knife holder that will probably be in that box.

Thinking about moves and moving reminded me of one of my more unpleasant memories. Mery worked with a woman, and one day, probably on a coffee break, they got into a discussion about moving. The woman was worried because they were moving, they were new to the area, and they didn't know anyone to help. Mery would have been sympathetic, maybe even in tears at the thought of strangers facing the moving chore alone. Had I been there, I would have nodded my head in sympathy and moved on to other topics (no play on words intended!). And I would have left the room as soon as the lady mentioned moving.

But Mery responded with her classic, "Dan loves . . ." And two days later, I showed up at the door of a couple I had never met. After brief introductions—Mery wasn't there because she had other obligations—the husband showed me the boxes stacked on the floor and the furniture that was going with them. Nothing looked that heavy. There was no mention of a refrigerator. And the couch was not a hated hide-a-bed (they should name that horrible piece of furniture the "break-a-back"). At the very least, the CPSC should require a warning label: "lifting this item may produce lifetime injury."

The husband—I think his name was Ralph, but it doesn't matter because I never saw him or them again—and I grabbed the kitchen table and threaded our way down the stairs. Ralph and his wife lived on the second floor, and that shouldn't have surprised me because I have never helped anyone move from ground floor to ground floor. People with ground-floor apartments seem to stay where they are. I asked Ralph where he had parked the truck.

"Didn't get one," Ralph told me without guilt and, surprising to me, even some pride. "Our new apartment is only two blocks away, so I figured we could just carry the stuff that far. We don't have that much." That easy move took most of my day. She served ham salad sandwiches for lunch, and like a surprisingly large number of people, I don't like ham salad. There is ham salad that is less bad than other versions, but there is no delicious ham salad. Please don't anyone send me your recipes for "Mom's great ham salad." And I mean no disrespect to anyone's mother. That tortuous move is still in my mind and will probably be one of my final thoughts when I depart this world. I suppose I should have just been grateful that it wasn't raining.

Forgetting all the moves I worked on, I want to mention something about truck rentals versus hiring a company, two mutually exclusive approaches to moving. I should have a more extended discussion on this topic, but I'm afraid that if I start talking about our experiences with moving companies, I will launch into an *unhinged diatribe*.

When I look at the ads showing people sitting in lawn chairs, sipping a drink, watching the smiling uniformed workers carrying obviously light boxes, and grinning at the people sitting in those chairs, I always wonder, *What planet are these people on?* Is there anyone who thinks those pictures of smiling people were taken during an actual move?

Now, about the physical act of moving, I would like to say that most of our experiences with our truck rentals have been positive, but I cannot. I would be lying through my teeth, although I have never understood that phrase. What does it mean to "lie through your teeth"? Is it possible to avoid your teeth entirely when you lie? Can you lie around your teeth?

If you have ever watched *Seinfeld*, and I am surprised when people tell me, "No, I never watched that show!" *What did you watch?* I want to yell. Anyway, they had a segment detailing Jerry's problem with a car rental agency and the car that he reserved not being there when he arrived. I love the line he used to the clerk who assured him that they knew all about reservations.

"I don't think you do," Jerry told her. "You see, you know how to *take* the reservation, you just don't know how to *hold* the reservation. And that's really the most important part of the reservation: the holding."

We found, to our dismay, and even Mery gets dismayed on occasion, that you might reserve a truck with this particular company, but that is no guarantee that you will get that size truck when you arrive at the counter. They will probably give you a truck if you have a reservation, but not necessarily the truck you wanted.

Whatever truck you get, well, you are going to need everyone's thoughts and prayers as you drive to your destination because there is every likelihood that the truck has already been beaten to a pulp. You may have the misfortune of driving the vehicle on its last trip. On our move to Michigan, our reservation for one large truck became two smaller ones, and as it turned out, my truck had major problems. I have been known to have bad karma. We spent five hours sitting outside another of the company's rental outlets, four hours from our destination, as they worked to repair the vehicle. That accursed vehicle had "died" as I attempted to accelerate onto the busy highway. They eventually fixed it, but as we pulled into our new driveway, nine hours past our expected arrival, the motor on my repaired truck was on fire. As I said, I have some bad karma.

And that was one of our better experiences. I still get a mental twinge similar to a brain freeze whenever we drive by that company's rental offices. I hope that negative feeling will eventually go away, but it may not. And I don't care because I will never darken their rental doors again.

Getting a reliable rental truck can be a problem, but that task is nothing compared to finding a reliable moving company. We heard all types of horror stories from people who had hired moving companies. They told us about instances where the company would not unload the furniture until the customer came up with an additional and often substantial payment. Friends told us about broken or chipped items coming off the truck and the careless manner in which their furniture was stacked in their new homes. Not many people—actually, I can't think of any—said that their moving company was "a delight to work with." Americans don't seem to be delighted much these days. Especially when they are moving. None of our friends could identify with those pictures of people sipping cold drinks as the smiling movers hauled the light boxes into the beautiful new homes.

We hired one of these professionals for our move to the retirement community. Our move was unusual because it had two parts. We were leaving our house and taking some stuff to Illinois, where we would be squatters at a friend's house for a month or two. Then, we would spend a couple of months at a downtown Asheville condo, but that date was indefinite because we weren't sure when we could move to our final destination.

Mery had organized the move. The boxes were labeled for content and which of the three destinations. But almost everything was going to a storage rental unit first—to one of three units. All three storage units were in the same complex, so this presumably was not difficult. And it was on the street level.

The moving company, through their representative doing the initial estimate, assured us that it would be no problem. He also professed to be amazed at Mery's organization. For the record, I did not buy into his amazement. Most of the heavier furniture, like our beloved refrigerator, stayed in the old house. This move, or so we thought at the time, was going to be a snap. I think Mery even had cookies for the moving crew. But we were on track to a major disappointment. Actually, more than one.

On the fateful moving day, the movers showed up more than two hours late, and they brought a small truck, far too small for our stuff. The driver and his crew of one, for some reason, thought our move involved only a few items. And they had another appointment at 1 p.m., so they had to hurry. Apparently, they never talked with the company's precision-trained estimator. That estimator took all those pictures that no one ever saw.

We explained—and by now, Mery had discarded any thought of cookies—how this was our last day, and we had to be out of the house. After emotional calls to their headquarters, the company sent another, longer truck. Great idea, finally, but this truck was too long for our steep driveway. We told the first representative about the steep driveway when he "estimated precisely" and snapped all the pictures. Apparently, his estimate and the pictures never arrived at headquarters. Or headquarters didn't care.

As a result, the workers had to carry the boxes and furniture down the steep driveway to the long truck that was now blocking our community's narrow access road. The roadblocks angered residents who lived in the community and had to get to work or wanted to go shopping. They were understandably frustrated, and their anger with the movers gave them a bad final feeling about us as we departed the neighborhood. We can still notice their grimaces when we come back for a visit. Mery is less attuned to negative vibes. I, on the other hand, grew up surrounded by negative vibes, so they don't bother me. But I do notice them.

The final affront to our sensibilities during this expensive, stage-one move was the disappearance of several boxes. It is difficult to understand how, in the transition from our house to the storage sheds, several important boxes and two lamps disappeared. Gone forever, something like the guy in the horror movie who is going to work and never arrives. And even the police can't figure it out. I mean in the movie, not our movers. We never called the police about our movers, but maybe we should have. Anyway, and naturally, Mom's china was not one of the lost items.

But at least I vented my considerable spleen against the movers. There is something about inserting a critical piece on Yelp that has you feeling better, like ointment on a paper cut. I have no data to back this up, but I am convinced that the same people who sell used cars or call you on the phone about your car warranty having expired eventually gravitate into the moving business.

Fortunately, there are good people in the business, and we located one of them for our final move. And wouldn't you know it, this time Mery didn't have any cookies. Anyway, all's well that ends well.

If you are moving and doing it yourself, make sure you have help. Tell your friends that you are cashing in on their IOUs for the times you helped them. And try to insist on a new truck, although anything less than 100,000 miles qualifies as new in this business. Remember that the people who rented that truck before you were just like you, with virtually no experience with a large vehicle, and probably abused the hell out of it.

And if you are using a professional, talk to individuals who have moved in the last year. Don't ask your brother-in-law who has a friend in the business, a guy who will give you a great deal.

Please don't call me. No matter what Mery might tell you, I don't like to help people move, and I have no desire to help anyone find a mover either. Besides, I now have a bad back. And if you think those events might be related, I think you might be right.

But all's well that ends well!

Dave:

We are getting closer to making the big move, and I am trying to focus on the advantages. You know me, the eternal optimist. One thing that appeals to me is that retirement community residents do not seem interested in anything other than enjoying themselves. How can that hedonistic attitude constitute anything but a good living environment?

And I feel sure there is room for people like me who want to be left alone to pursue their own interests. Sometimes the main obstacle to "retirement living" is the negative image or stereotypes people have. Including me, I hate to say. Even after thirty years of studying this segment of the life cycle, I have this profound reluctance to think about living in an age-centered setting because, among other things, I see retirement communities as elephant burial grounds, where these magnificent animals go to die.

And understandably, people hate the idea that they are getting ready to die. Many of us think that we are just getting started. But of course, we are not; our ending is far closer than our beginning.

So, I will leave you with that image, me (sans tusks) walking slowly into the sunset while Tarzan (you) is watching me trudge into the setting sun, knowing that the process is sad but natural and inevitable, and he (you) will not see me again. And then you grab a vine, which for some reason always seems right there, hanging on the tree next to your arm, and you swing off to another rousing sexual encounter with Jane, who is making oyster stew for dinner.

Meanwhile, I am trudging with considerable effort to the burial ground, looking for support that never

comes. It doesn't seem fair.
   Keep in touch. While you can!
Dan

4.

First Impressions of Our New Home

After the many visits and tours, sampling various, sometimes tasty snacks with sales representatives from the retirement communities and housing clusters in the Asheville area, we finally selected *The Home*—a place where we were going to live for the rest of our lives. That term, "final home," sounds so absolute, even ominous, and I suppose it should. Like that recorded message telling me that my car's extended warranty had expired and I only had until the end of the month to renew it, and they weren't responsible if something bad happened to that car with me in it.

I would be interested in finding out how many people respond to those periodic robocalls about their cars. Do any Americans really believe that their files just landed on this guy's desk, and he is genuinely concerned about their lapsed warranties? And that he felt the overwhelming need to call them? I think it was Mencken who said that no one ever went broke underestimating the intelligence of the American people, and that was a long time ago. Maybe we haven't progressed as much as we would like to think.

Anyway, after we picked our new community, we selected a two-bedroom apartment with a view of trees because it seemed to be everything we wanted, and because it was available. The waiting time for the houses we liked more was, at the time, about three years. Mery wasn't positive I had three years left, and at that point, neither was I. Advancing age along with a traumatic relocation can give you a fatalistic perspective.

Where should I begin to describe my initial impressions of the home? It is fascinating how often we encounter that phrase, "Where do I begin?" It makes you wonder, *Why is he starting with such an asinine question?* Wherever you start will be the beginning, and if you had a problem determining your jumping-off point and are worried you might start in the middle of a long story and have to backtrack, you haven't thought enough about your topic.

That critique may apply in some instances, but not here. I know the best place to begin. Why do I refer to our new retirement setting as "The Home"? Over the years, whenever Mery and I would argue about something, like whether the house needed painting or if I needed to flip the mattress, I would summarize my failed opposition by saying, "Well, at least I won't have to worry about this when we go to *The Home!*"

The phrase got to be a running joke, and our friends and neighbors picked up on it. When we started looking at retirement communities, it seemed natural for me to refer to them as "The Home." I felt like a guy driving a covered wagon for months, and then, at the crest of a hill, he looked down on this lush valley with a stream running through it and got excited. The guy, often played by Kevin Costner or Ward Bond, looked in the back of the wagon where his wife sleeps with their new baby and yelled, "Honey, we're home!"

Whenever I watched a scene like that, I couldn't help but wonder how the guy decided that no one already lived in that lush valley. And if someone already lived there, was he going to tell his honey, now on the verge of hysterics, that "No, I guess this isn't it. But we're close!"

Mery is less tolerant now when I use the term "The Home" and admonishes me if I use it in public. "Do you have to describe our new apartment that way?" Then she'll turn to our companions and assure them I was just kidding. She is very good at admonishing because she had considerable admonishment training as a teacher. But I suspect it could also be a genetic trait. Her grandmother and mother could reduce people to tears when they admonished.

But I am now in the habit of saying *The Home,* and old habits are difficult to break. A logical place to start with my impressions is the food. The meals were one of the first things that stuck in my mind, although I probably should find a word other than "stuck" when I discuss institutional food. Food quality is always a question people have when they want to know about your vacation, cities you visited, or even visits to relatives. "How was the food? What did they give you for dinner? Did that include homemade rolls?"

People want to know what you ate, how much of it, and how you reacted. The type and quality of food is important to people. As it should be. Many thick books have been written about the role food has played in cultures throughout history. Ancient Rome, for example, did not begin their disastrous decline until their wine went bad. Anyway, that's what some historians claim.

It's important to point out that American pioneers used food and water quality as the basis for selecting their spots to settle. "It's got good water here, cold and crystal clear." That sounds like the kind of comment that might make the wife feel better when she saw the Native Americans scowling about the new farm encroaching on traditional hunting grounds. When we were looking at retirement places, we always asked about the food, but mostly as a conversational topic. But we both knew that food quality was on our minds.

On our first day at The Home, someone asked about my military service. "Were you in the army?" I don't know why the question came up because I wasn't wearing my old uniform, and I don't wear one of those caps. And it wasn't Veteran's Day. Maybe she was just trying to start a conversation. Whatever the motivation, she asked me what I thought of army food. Every time someone asks that question, I have to think about how long or short my answer should be. I could provide a long response because it's a complex topic. But people don't usually want long answers.

For example, when someone asks you, "How are you doing?" what they expect is a concise answer that will permit them to go on to other things. Or maybe to other people. "How are you doing" is another throwaway phrase, the kind you toss out on your way to somewhere else.

The routine response is, "Fine, thanks." Or, if you want a bit of humor, you might say, "Well, I managed to dress myself this morning." Then you chuckle and plan on moving on to other topics, but the guy who asked how you were doing is already two tables away and didn't hear your pithy remark.

Every so often, you encounter an individual who regards your query as a license to tell you about everything that happened that day and maybe include a description of his physical ailments and various treatments he is trying for those conditions. Somewhere in the middle of this extended narrative, your mind will wander, and you will be looking for an outlet.

I spent three wonderful years in the army. I'm kidding about that experience being wonderful, but now that I look back, it wasn't so bad. It seems that everything gets better, or at least less bad, over time. Memory is a great emotional salve. It always has been for me. I can even talk about my dental appointments without breaking into a cold sweat. Unless you ask about my implants.

Anyway, during my enlistment, I spent considerable time in two countries and lived on five different army bases. The food was bad to varying degrees in each place, so my short answer is, "Not very good." Or if I am in a humorous mood, I might say, "I'm still here, so I guess it wasn't that bad." When I find people who recently left the army, they often insist, "Well, the food is a lot better now."

Maybe it is! Or maybe expectations have changed. But either way, they don't know about my experiences. I find it hard to believe that any organization that selected their cooks from the ranks—well, soldier, you can't seem to get the hang of driving a tank, so I guess you're going to be our new cook—is ever going to produce good meals.

I remember returning from a five-week trip to what was then the Soviet Union. I had some incredible experiences there, including a visit to the Hermitage Museum. But the first, and sometimes only, question people asked was, "Was the food any good?" By the way, it wasn't. If I had to pick between eating dinner in an army mess hall or a Russian restaurant, I would probably skip the meal entirely and eat a big breakfast the next morning. There are good reasons why we see so few Russian restaurants in our cities. Lebanese, French, lots of Italian, there are even a few English pubs with fish and chips, probably the only English dish that Americans find appealing. But you have to look hard to find a Russian restaurant.

And if you were wondering why they use the term "mess hall"—and if you weren't, you could have been—from what I found in my cursory search, the term apparently started in the Middle Ages, when soldiers and sailors would describe their bug-infested meals as "a mess." There is a good reason, then, why the term persisted. But to be fair, I don't remember any of my army meals that were bug-infested.

Well then, what is the food like at The Home? First, a disclaimer; well, more like a qualifier. People, my wife especially, sometimes describe me as a "picky eater," and I suppose I am, although I have never considered myself picky. But it is difficult for me to eat with any enthusiasm when I dislike the taste. And I suppose that I don't like the taste of that many foods.

I used to be polite and would try to eat even if I didn't like what was on my plate. But over the years, I stopped trying. And if I cook a big meal and a guest says, "What is in this casserole? I can't eat this," I'm fine with that. A friend of ours was at the other end of the food politeness continuum. At a dinner party we all attended, the food was outrageously bad. But my friend asked for seconds, and when I asked him about it later, he told me, "It was the polite thing to do." I am not that polite. Not even close. When people notice the food on my plate at the end of a meal—and some people watch for such things—Mery will shake her head and say, "He has always been a picky eater." And so, the "picky" legend takes root.

In fairness to me, I do try to be more accommodating when we go to someone's home. When you get invited for dinner, people usually feed you one of their "special dishes." And it always worries me when someone says, "Wait until Dan tastes my kale loaf. He is going to love it." That is a lot of pressure when you eat. If it turns out that your first bite of the special kale loaf reminds you of cough medicine, you know it's going to be a long and difficult meal.

And my experience in these episodes of signature dishes is that I should not look forward to dessert. They may serve me another special dish, something like pecan pie, which I don't like, or even worse, their homemade banana bread, and no matter who bakes this concoction, I won't like it. The heaviness of that concoction can remain in my stomach for days. And I speak here from years of painful experiences with this dish.

I have never liked anyone's banana bread, and personally, I wish every person I know would stop baking or buying it. The same goes for pecan pie. Even though every bookstore has shelves of cookbooks, some actually good, I don't recall any cookbook devoted to "dishes you might want to avoid serving to your guests." This might be a great idea for a book if anyone is looking for good cookbook ideas.

Dining at a friend's house can be a delicate dinner affair, especially if the hosts are good friends. Bread has been my savior in these cases—obviously not banana bread! If I have trouble with the kale loaf, I can claim to have "filled up on bread" and also use it to cover the leftovers I am returning to the kitchen. If neither of these options is feasible or believable, I will fall back on the standard explanation: "Sorry, but I'm nursing a weak stomach." Few people want to contend with upsetting a guest's tender stomach. The weak stomach is better than the more honest, "Sorry, but this banana bread tastes like shit."

Our new retirement home has tried its best to service people like me, and I will say that they have made a credible effort. (And how's that for writing a lot of words but saying nothing?) Here at The

Home, they provide alternatives for the main courses at every meal. If I do not like the daily main course, I have options. It's not like the army where you had the meal loaded onto your metal tray, and it was eat or starve. Sometimes, starving seemed like the best idea.

As a general rule, I think the side dishes at The Home tend to be slightly undercooked, and the main dishes are just the opposite. But the main dishes change every day, and that is usually a good thing. You can also use the salad bar to build an appealing salad and select from two soups that may or may not be good that day. And there is a pizza oven. The pizzas are pretty decent. I have been told that the director of food services went to several local pizza joints until he found the best pizza. Then he offered the cook a job. That narrative may not be true, but it is a good story.

There is also a grill at The Home that provides hamburgers, with your choice of condiments and weekly special sandwiches. A few weeks ago, they were making Reubens. I got one and didn't like it, but you can't make too much of this because I don't like Reubens. I am not trying to abuse myself with my food choices, but on that day, the Reuben seemed my best option.

The dining service has three restaurants. There is some overlap with hours, but the smallest facility generally serves breakfast and lunch and has a limited menu. But the breakfast and lunch sandwiches we ate there were excellent, as were their varied pastries. And then there is the more upscale restaurant, also with a limited, though mostly excellent, dinner menu.

Overall, I give the dining service here a "C+." And from me, that is significant praise. The quality and selection are better than I expected. I can imagine the difficulties in trying to satisfy the wants and needs of 900 demanding customers; the staff say they are trying to make their product even better, and I never heard any army cooks say that. And I think that is enough about food!

Housing here at The Home includes options, and that selection attracted us. Individual homes of varying sizes, duplexes, and high-rise buildings were all built with an eye for visual appeal. The designs changed as the administration evaluated the appeal and the costs. The earlier high-rise structures used the first or basement level for resident parking. This design worked out well, and residents with the inside parking slots seem happy with the arrangement even though they had to pay for the parking privilege. But the administration abandoned that parking feature in the newer high-rises, apparently because of cost.

The earlier high-rises also had meeting rooms, public restrooms, and open areas for resident gatherings. But these amenities also disappeared in the newer structures, which is where we eventually moved. More than a few residents referred to our new buildings as "low-income housing."

Speaking of restrooms, the American perspective on public restrooms has, sadly, changed over the years. Our industrial society does not seem to think it important to provide places for the public to relieve their toilet urges. I read an article a few years ago that attempted to explain the "disappearing public washrooms." Anyone who wanders through the nation's downtown areas can attest to that uncomfortable situation. More than once, we went into a city's downtown restaurant and ordered sandwiches we didn't want so that we could use the restroom. Even many gas stations, the traditional oases for public bathrooms, have signs stating that "our bathrooms are only for customers." What kind of organization refuses bathroom privileges to a person who has to pee, even if they don't buy gas?

I loved the public restrooms in downtown Copenhagen, Denmark. You put a coin in the slot, and I don't remember it being much money, although when you travel, the local currency always seems a little like Monopoly money. Two hundred krona for this coconut donut? No problem. Give me three of them.

Back to the Danish restroom! You use the facility, and when you leave, the door shuts, and a blast of steam cleans the facility from top to bottom. Everyone seems happy with the arrangement. I know I was. I could wander through beautiful Copenhagen, secure in the knowledge that I could use a restroom as long as I had a few coins in my pocket.

Our new apartment building is beautiful from the outside and has some attractive internal features. No public restrooms, though! We do have the convenience of an inside mailroom and a garbage room.

This is Mery's first experience in apartment living, but I grew up in Chicago apartments, so the inevitable sounds from neighbors don't bother me. When you live in an apartment, your ceiling is another resident's floor. When your upstairs neighbors walk, run, or dance on the floor, you are likely to hear some noise.

I still remember the older lady upstairs in one of our Chicago apartments. Mrs. Janke seemed older to me then, but maybe she was only in her forties. Every time I practiced my accordion, she would rap on her floor. On our ceiling! It was usually when I was playing, or trying to play, that German love song, *"Du, du liegst mir im Herzen."* I thought she was so taken emotionally with my playing that she wanted me to play it louder, and I usually did. But now, I suspect she was begging me to stop.

As the new residents adjusted to their sometimes dramatically different lifestyles, some of them complained that they "never see anyone." They probably didn't know it, but their complaints demonstrate what sociologists describe as the "high-rise syndrome." People have made similar complaints about high-rise living since there have been high rises, although I doubt whether that information would comfort our new neighbors.

Multilevel buildings might be efficient and impressive to look at, but they can be difficult places to live if you are a sociable person and want to meet your neighbors. On the other hand, if you are a private person, high-rise living will not present any social problems. The reason for this persistent lack of contact with neighbors is the absence of community space. High-rise residents live in their apartments, and that apartment is their home. Not the building, not the hallway, just the apartment!

The road to their apartment, the hallway, is almost foreboding ground, similar to the dark street in front of your house or the alley behind your house. And that might be the best description of high-rise hallways. They are your building's alleys!

When you come into your building carrying two bags of groceries, your goal is to get into your safe space, into your apartment, as quickly as possible. You don't linger in the hallways or even the mailroom because you don't belong there. You may even feel uneasy standing in front of someone's mailbox, and you want to get out of there as fast as you can.

I remember our first week, standing in the hall, when a resident opened her door, obviously planning to go somewhere. When she saw us in front of her door, she got this "deer in the headlights" look on her face, apologized, although there was no need for an apology, and shut the door. I think she may have slammed it. She didn't open it again until we had gone. I'm not sure she ever opened her door again without looking through her peephole first. And not incidentally, all the apartment doors in the new building have these "peepholes."

Many residents in newer suburban developments have similar complaints about not meeting anyone. And they had complaints about "unfriendly neighbors." It didn't take long for astute social scientists to isolate the problem. This speed was a little unusual because it normally takes a good deal of time for social scientists to pinpoint even obvious social patterns. Anyway, the suburban developments were built without front porches. As a result, suburban residents spent their free time in their backyards, sipping lemonade on the back decks and watching their dogs running around.

It seems obvious that you have fewer chances to get acquainted when there are no front porches. Maybe it is, but only to sociologists. Meanwhile, the residents will continue to complain about the unfriendly neighborhoods.

In my Chicago South Side neighborhood, virtually every house had a front porch. They were not large porches; they couldn't be because the houses were not large, but they provided a location where homeowners sat and waved to neighbors, where they talked to people walking by, sometimes with their dogs, and where their kids sold lemonade. But in the suburbs of today, there are no front porches, no more waving to neighbors, no more lemonade stands, and fewer friendly neighbors.

I noticed other unusual features in our new apartment. None of the apartment interior doors had locks. Not even the bathrooms, and as far as I am concerned, a bathroom door without a lock is bad for everyone. Haven't we all experienced the frustration and embarrassment of someone opening the bathroom door, seeing us on the toilet, then yelling, "Why didn't you lock the door?"

Our front doors also have no security chains or bolt locks. Again, maybe it is my history of living in Chicago, but I take comfort in being able to lock my front door, even if the lock is less than massive. My guess is that resident safety would be the explanation for the absence of locks, but someone should ask if safety trumps privacy. Another interesting research question!

And that general notion about safety is doubtlessly also the reason for the plethora (always been one of my favorite words!) of smoke detectors in the new apartments. And the explanation for the regular appearance of the community fire trucks. Burn the bacon, forget to take the frying pan off the stove, put a little too much oil in the skillet, and you are going to be saying another sheepish hello to the local firefighters. I wish I could listen to the conversations they had on their way back to the station after they responded, again, to burning bacon in a senior apartment.

Safety concerns appear to be behind the coming changes to the entrance of the property. An informal guard shack will be updated, and entrance gates will be installed. No one will be getting onto the property without a sticker on their car or a legitimate reason for entry. Security personnel will be wandering the grounds, looking for problems or sinister intruders.

In my mind, the residents are probably watching too much television. Studies consistently show that the more television we watch, the more worried we will be about crime, rampaging immigrant hoards, and government seizure of our automatic weapons. Maybe they should put a lid on television watching or a safety lock on programs residents can watch, but that is not likely. But if residents spent their viewing hours watching reruns of *Mr. Rogers* rather than *Tucker Carlson*, we would not have so much emphasis on security concerns.

There was another issue right after we arrived, one that involved dogs, not sinister intruders. Apparently, they had some problems with residents not cleaning up after their dogs. The classic straw that broke someone's back was when one of the staff stepped in poop while wearing new shoes.

Had anyone asked me, I would have said it is no big deal to have dog poop on your shoes. We had golden retrievers in our homes for thirty years, and it was impossible to walk outside without stepping in poop. And in case you can't visualize it, believe me, golden retriever poop is good-sized. Our lawn looked like Johnny Bratwurst had been scattering his sausages.

I always washed the bottoms of my shoes before going inside, but believe me, poop gets hard after a few hours and stays on your shoes until you scrape it off with something like a putty knife. After a few years, you just come to accept dog poop as a part of your life. But the administration here wasn't going to wait.

No one in the management ranks seriously considered banning dogs. That could have started a revolution here. What someone thought of as the best alternative to a dog banning was to register the DNA of all the dogs. Residents who had dogs were required to bring the dogs in for a mouth swab. And then they were reminded to clean up after their dogs because severe penalties were in the works.

Then the next time dog poop was discovered on a trail, on the sidewalk, or inside the mailroom, a call was made, and a staff member, probably one of the new personnel, came, scooped up the poop, and took it back to some sort of laboratory. They ran a DNA test on the poop to locate the offender. Hefty fines were levied. The effectiveness of this program has yet to be determined.

No one has made any policy statement as yet about whether it is permissible for dogs to relieve themselves in the woods. If the dogs go in the woods, I don't see that as a problem. If it comes up in a conversation, I intend to throw out the classic philosophical question, *Does a bear shit in the woods?* The issue has not yet come up, but I look forward to posing that classical question.

Another feature that impressed me—actually, I can't say that because that statement implies I think it was a good thing, and I don't—is the vast and growing administrative structure here, a virtual cobweb of groups, clusters, and committees spanning topics and issues from food service to placement of planting boxes.

Like other organizations in the country focused on elderly housing, this community is administered by professionals who seem to know their business. Or they assure us that they do. And someone in that managerial assembly decided it made sense to establish an enormous number of "resident advisory groups" that advise the professional managers. How often and how seriously the administration takes this advice, I don't know. What do you call advice that no one wants?

Many years ago, when I first started researching housing for older citizens, I wrote about the presence—and absence—of resident councils. And although I hesitate to quote myself because it sounds self-serving, and it probably is, I need to make the point that I am not against resident councils. This is what I wrote in 1982: "The single best indicator of such involvement would be the existence of a resident council . . . although the mere existence is in itself not a sufficient basis for concluding that the residents have some control over their environment." My cogent analysis cited a series of studies showing that the traditional dominance of the administration and staff often continued despite the existence of resident councils.

The situation here with the various resident groups is similar to many university's relationships with student groups. Universities insist that they are interested in what students think. But you never would know it from what they did—or what they did not do—with the input from student groups.

It is too early to make definitive assessments about the effectiveness of the resident groups here. But I am amazed at how many groups there are, holding meetings, taking notes, issuing summaries, and making recommendations. As a resident, it would be possible, if that was your intention, to spend most of your days attending meetings, reading the notes from previous meetings, or planning for your next meeting. That type of mostly meaningless group activity during the last few years of my academic life drove me up a wall, although I don't know exactly what that phrase means. But I have noticed a few drivers here who may provide me with a specific illustration soon.

Mery did not spend her career as I did in the labyrinths of higher education, so she does not share my disdain for committee activity. She seems to thrive on her committee work. She always seems to be attending a meeting, reading the minutes from meetings she attended, or agonizing over the meetings she missed; she maintains a weekly calendar that would rival that of a corporate executive. It is intriguing for me to watch her sitting with another active resident, comparing calendars, and scheduling another meeting that will not conflict with someone else's planned meeting. My mind spins when I watch them.

After a few months here, when we go to the dining room and I search, sometimes in vain, for something I would like to eat, Mery will wave at people so often that her meal gets cold. When residents approach her to discuss the next meeting of some obscure group, they often look over at me, smile, and say, "I'm sorry. I don't think we've met." They are embarrassed when they discover that I am the husband, but they shouldn't be; we probably haven't met, not unless they somehow snuck into our apartment and saw me sitting at my desk.

This pattern is not new. When we lived in Michigan, Mery was deeply involved in that mostly rural community; I was deeply involved in our yard, my writing, and our dogs, not necessarily in that order. On one occasion, she was marching with her kazoo band in the town's July Fourth bash. I am not a fan of parades or kazoos, for that matter, so I was going to skip the event and take our dogs for an extended stroll in the woods. She asked me if I would be willing to come downtown and take a few pictures of the band for the local newsletter.

It was a nice day, so I delayed the dog walk, jumped on my bike—well, I got on my bike; I haven't jumped on my bike for many years—and rode to town. When the parade started, it was only three or four floats because ours was a small town with only one gas station and one restaurant. There were two restaurants at one time, but the second one closed, and that building is still vacant.

I got off my bike and edged into the street to get a few pictures of the pathetically small kazoo band. Suddenly, a voice boomed out from behind me. "Do you mind moving? I'm trying to get a picture of my friend, Mery, and you're in the way." I think that comment says it all.

Back to the present, if I were to list the important items in assessing the quality of a residential living environment, the first and most important item would be the staff. Who are the staff? Do they seem happy in their work? What kind of interaction do they have with residents? Is there a high turnover?

We haven't been here long enough to answer all these questions, but so far, I am impressed. The staff seem courteous in responding to even outrageous requests, they are patient with residents, and they are prompt with service requests. Mery recently filled out a work order to have a few dimmers installed in our house lights. This is a task I would normally do, but not here. As one employee told us, "This is what we are here for."

I have heard nothing but praise from residents about the staff. There is an annual event here—the staff appreciation lunch—that says a lot. Volunteer residents make lunch for the staff—cookies, salads, dips, and sandwiches—and serve them to the staff.

At this same event, they also have an awards ceremony, and staff members each receive a check from a fund donated by residents. Obviously, I was not on that committee, but I understand that the amount was based on how long the employee had been with the organization. Other than the committee members, none of us knows exactly how much was given to each employee, but judging from the reactions, the checks were fairly significant. More than anything, though, the awards and the luncheon are a good index for the positive feelings residents have about the staff.

On the other hand, though, staff turnover here is high, around 40 percent. That makes life more difficult for the remaining staff and the residents. The favorable job market may account for the high turnover, though, at least in part, and not necessarily a dislike for their jobs.

Another process I observed during my earlier research in elderly housing was what social scientists describe as "nonperson treatment." The *nonperson* process refers to workers or administrators who ignore the feelings or presence of residents, in effect treating residents as though they were not important in any discussions. Nonperson treatment is not exclusive to older people. Most of us have experienced it on a job, as students, or while standing in line for service from an organization not known for polite customer service. The electric company is one example of a company that "excels" at nonperson treatment. It is comforting that they excel at something.

I have not observed any of this nonperson treatment here. And that also speaks well for this organization and the people who work here. If the residents are treated as individuals by the staff, and if the reverse is also true, then you have the makings of a positive working and living environment. But there is an "on the other hand" here. Several residents have expressed their frustrations about complaining to higher administrators. One lady said she was so frustrated that she told one administrator she was going to move. "Where are you going to go?" he dismissively replied. Another resident said that her complaints about repairs were met with muted laughter as the workers were talking, apparently, about other things, on the sidewalk in front of her home.

Overall, though, as we move toward our first anniversary here, *The Home* has not been a bad place to live. I'm getting accustomed to the different lifestyle, living in an apartment with no private backyard and greeting a large number of people on our way to and from dinner. I discovered that even individuals like myself, with a slightly off-center perspective and a preference for privacy, can be reasonably comfortable in a congregate living environment.

Dave:

We are having a major rainstorm right now, what we in the south refer to as a "gully washer," but I suppose that you have no idea of what a "gully washer" is, and I have no desire to take the time and space to define the term. So let me modify that description and say, "Holy shit, it is raining hard here today."

I told Mery I didn't want to walk to The Home's restaurant to get today's dinner, ham steak with bourbon glaze and dilled potatoes. What does that mean, Dave, "dilled potatoes"? If you sprinkle salt on your potatoes, can you describe them as "salted potatoes"? Be that as it may, which it rarely is anymore, if you put your vegetables in a blender, they all taste the same.

But I thought I would give you the details of what happened this morning before you hear it on CNN. Ha, ha, got you there. I don't think this will be on CNN, although it has been a slow news cycle. So it might be.

Anyway, we were milling around this morning, and I was nursing my wounds from the skin cancer operation yesterday. I have a hole in my upper lip that resembles a third nostril. But my dermatologist—I have never understood why people persist in using that pronoun when talking about their medical providers. The proper designation is "*the* dermatologist." She is certainly not, nor has she ever been, "mine." Although she is a nice person, worth keeping if that notion is appropriate. Which it is definitely not.

Where was I? Anyway, I asked Mery if she might be interested in a hard-boiled egg. "Sure, and you might as well boil the rest of them so we can have egg salad for lunch later in the week." Mery has always been a long-distance thinker.

I put a water on to boil and moved to other household chores. Several minutes later, Mery looked up from her laptop computer and remarked, "I hear a crackling sound from the stove."

I thought it was the water boiling, but when I looked over, a small butter dish was sitting over the burner that I had inadvertently turned on. In my defense, electric ranges can be very deceptive! You never know which burner you turned on because all that stove panel shows you is a diagram and an arrow, and then some of them have a large and small burner on the same spot, so you have to be careful that you are turning the knob in the proper direction. Yee gods!

I ran over and pulled the butter dish away. But this elegant butter dish also had a plastic rim that enabled you to put the butter into a neat slot. And it was this plastic that started to smoke. I turned the stove vent on and thought my decisive move solved the smoke problem. I did not, however, foresee the sensitivity of the smoke alarms in our housing unit.

Suddenly, the ear-splitting fire alarms go off. And I think I understand now what the term "ear-splitting" means. We opened the windows and turned on the ceiling fans and assumed that this would deal with the situation. We also called the number in our resident manual and told them there was no problem. But unfortunately, the alarm continued to split our ears.

Then a big fire truck pulled in front of the apartment, followed by not one but two more large trucks. And then, of course, with that many trucks and firemen, you need a battalion chief. His red SUV pulled up shortly thereafter. He wore a white helmet; the other helmets were black.

Firemen poured into the hallway. I went out there

to assure them there was no problem, that it was just a butter dish, but I was told by a fireman who could easily have been on the 911 show, "Sorry, sir, we have to check it out." Six of them came into our apartment, but it seemed like more with all the equipment they carried. After they assured themselves that there was no active fire, they accepted my apologies and left. And they finally shut the damn, ear-splitting alarm off.

Now that kind of smoke event in any of our earlier domiciles would have been no big deal. And no ear-splitting alarm. But now, in some chart I'm sure they are keeping on the occupants of our housing unit, they probably have a note to "check on the cooking habits of the residents in apt. 203."

My cooking error has not yet made it into the *Resident Gazette*, but this is only the first day. And if the truth be told, which, as we know, it rarely is, this is the real reason I am not going down for the ham steak with dilled potatoes. I feel as though I am wearing a scarlet letter "F" (for Fuck-Up). That fire alarm went off just after 7 a.m., and I have no doubt that some residents were just turning over in bed. They will not take kindly to the disturbance and will be looking for the culprit.

You are now up to date.

Dan

5.

Our Long-Standing Marital Treaty: Now Null and Void!

I always wondered why those similar terms, null and void, are so often linked. If something is null, then presumably, it will be voided. The extra word sounds like something a lawyer would have added, like making a contract hard and fast, final, and complete, over and done.

Mery and I established ground rules early in the marriage. We knew there were going to be routine disagreements because we had listened to married people who argued a lot. They debated whose turn it was to take out the garbage, shovel the sidewalk, or walk the dog, although at least we didn't have any dogs to argue about yet. This was a time when significant changes in marital roles were emerging and an exciting time to be a newlywed. We felt as though we were helping to carve new trails in the thick marital forest.

If you got married in the 1960s, you no longer expected that the wife was going to do all the cooking and shopping, and she would not be looking for you to do furnace and car repairs. The magazines from the forties and fifties are almost comical and maybe even a little offensive by the standards of today. As an example, one ad for a new electric iron was captioned, "Give her something to ease her workload."

Another interesting ad from that period urged women to "make the house clean for him when he comes home after a hard day." That ad was for a vacuum cleaner. How far we have come! But that feeling about social progress depends on perspective. Some people might say, "Look how far we have fallen."

I don't think there is any way of going back to what some Americans might describe as "the good old days." I found a copy of our first treaty, and our marital innocence was almost cute. We hadn't confronted the more serious issues yet, but they would come later. Boy, would they! As that second-year document showed, I wanted Mery to stop making so many plans because I wanted more spontaneity in our lives. And I wanted her to stop wearing my pajamas.

She wanted me to try being more agreeable to her social planning and work on my fetishes about what constituted proper clothing. Obviously, there were already signs of basic differences, but I don't think we recognized them right away. But we would.

Our positions crystallized—maybe hardened would be a better description. We adjusted as best we could to the other person's behavior.

After futile attempts to come to an agreement about the "activities of daily living," we decided that we needed basic principles instead of specific rules; otherwise, we would be confronting one another every day about routine matters that didn't really *matter*. We didn't want to spend time arguing about garbage pickups and paint colors. At least I didn't.

We developed the outlines for a basic treaty, constructed a document, and reached an understanding that guided us from that point. Unlike ponderous government documents, our treaty was short and simple; any change inside the home was her domain. I would have the opportunity to express an opinion, but Mery had the final say with any internal home disputes. The agreement meant that we sometimes ended up with furniture or wall paint that offended my sensibilities, but such is the nature of treaties. You give a little, and you get a little. Although I think Native Americans might argue the truth in that statement.

And that would be a good way to describe my involvement with matters inside the house—getting a little. On occasion, I would come home and be confronted with a new piece of furniture or arrangement of existing furniture. Sometimes, I had no problem with it. But if I did, I would be reminded that she "had complete authority for the inside of the house."

Sometimes, the new furniture arrangement was not to my liking. After some of the changes, on my early morning walk to the bathroom, I might trip over furniture that had not been there the night before. But you adjust, or you perish. Such is the nature of the marital world.

And I had the entire outside world as my domain! At first blush, that arrangement appears slanted in my favor, with Mery's interests restricted to the 1,500 square feet in the house while I had everything else—in other words, the rest of the known universe.

Although there is an apparent disparity in areas of responsibility, that disparity is nowhere near as large as it appears. Asheville, for example, would obviously not be responsive to any suggestions I made about new housing developments, and I doubt they would be impressed by our treaty. What seemed, at first, to be a disparity was definitely not. My vast authority realistically extended only to the confines of our backyards.

But I ruled my domains with a perspective that some observers might describe as ruthless. I know that a few of Mery's friends described it that way because I saw them whispering and throwing critical glances in my direction. After a group of them went shopping for potted flowers and life-sized plastic statues of St. Francis suitable for a garden, I found out they wondered why Mery did not buy anything; she explained the treaty and that she "would have to check with Dan about planting flowers or getting that beautiful owl statue."

And she did check, and her periodic entreaties mostly went nowhere. Actually, they always went nowhere! I am a minimalist with the outdoors. I prefer to let nature do her work. I kept invasive weeds away from the house, trimmed limbs back from the house, and prevented pine needles from eating our roof, but I was mostly a casual observer and admirer of nature's works.

I was especially hostile to the idea of planting flowers around the house. I had no intention of letting our log house look like the entrance to a flower store. In my mind, we lived in a log house in the middle of the woods, and that is what I wanted it to look like. And it did.

Mery was not always happy with the outside, but she was not willing to abrogate our treaty. This understanding didn't stop her from walking through the garden sections of Lowe's and Home Depot with the haunting expression of a kid in a candy shop. She loves flowers, especially daisies, and she was intrigued by the displays of new bubbling fountain sculptures. But I stood firm; if you insist on hearing running water, I told her, turn on our kitchen faucets.

We had other challenges to the treaty, especially after we left our spacious wooded property in Illinois and moved to Asheville. After more than twenty years of country life, we then had a fairly large city lot but a smaller house and garage. We faced frequent confrontations over areas that were ignored earlier in our lives: Is a covered porch inside or outside the house? Who has jurisdiction over a porch? I thought I did. She thought she did.

What about the uncovered deck? The deck is obviously outside, exposed to the elements, but it is also attached to the house. We both claimed the deck. Such were the jurisdictional disputes that we never settled satisfactorily. We consulted our friends, but their biased opinions failed to sway either of us.

For the first time in our marriage, we had an attached garage in Asheville. Does this attachment make the garage part of the house? The Asheville garage became an ongoing territorial battleground; it was part of the house, but I still considered it mine, a place for garden tools, gas cans, screwdrivers, and nails.

We never really settled the disputes. Usually, after a craft fair—

Asheville seems to have them with depressing regularity—I would come home and find an unusual statue on the deck. "I found that at the craft fair," she'd explain, as though that justified her treaty violation. And we never established the penalties for a treaty violation. Rules and treaties mean nothing without accountability. Our society has experienced instances where people don't care about the rules; they only know what they want. And such disregard for rules never turns out well.

That "me attitude" was apparent during the prohibition years in the US. Outlawing alcohol was a disaster by any measure. Many Americans didn't care what the government and Elliot Ness said; if Americans wanted a beer, and many of them did, they were going to have a beer. And usually more than one. That dismissive attitude about laws produced a criminal enterprise during the 1920s that is still with us. I brought that historical episode to Mery's attention when she committed what I thought of as a treaty violation, but we never brought a violation case to trial. I'm not sure where we would've taken it or who would have selected the judge.

But when we moved to our new home, our long-standing treaty, that bulwark against so many arguments, a document negotiated through streams of sweat and tears, was null and void. Let's just say it was voided. The treaty had to be voided since our environment had altered in a major way. Our new living space was now encased in sheets of plasterboard, an entry door, and four internal sliding doors. There was no longer any "outside" domain. But Mery had no problems with my absence of territory and no sympathy when she told me, "You were getting tired of doing yard work anyway!" I have no proof, but I suspect that she enjoyed watching me squirm, devoid of any property rights, with no garden implements to sharpen, no tractor to drive around the property, no massive snowblower, and no garage to store any of the things I didn't have anyway.

With the practiced eye of a social scientist, I observed couples who have lived here for a few years, and I am guessing that many of them had similar adjustment issues. Moving from a home to a different kind of environment, especially one without a yard and a garage, was difficult, especially if you're accustomed to machines. On more than one occasion, I saw one or two of my new neighbors in the local hardware store, just staring at the power tools.

There was another process affected by our major move: furniture shopping. After you move into a home—or in our case, The Home—you have usually downsized and have no need to shop for furniture. Furniture shopping is a skill, but you may not be good at it anymore. We don't remember how to deal with pushy salespeople or how to negotiate for lower prices, and we lost our ability to express indignation about the delivery charges. "What? I have to pay extra for delivery?" Feigning indignation is an essential shopping skill.

Furniture shopping is not like riding a bicycle. It must be learned and nurtured, like playing the accordion, and you can easily forget what you thought you knew. I was never any good at it. Accordion playing, I mean! I enjoy shopping for furniture as much as most guys, which is to say, not at all. I remember many expressions on men's faces in furniture stores, their apparent pain and suffering. A couple of times, I've asked, "Having fun?" We shared a momentary chuckle, probably our only laughs of the day.

If I furniture shopped alone, the purchase would never take more than an hour. Probably a lot less. I think what I do should be called "buying" because I do very little "shopping," If left to my own inclinations, which, of course, I never am, I would go into a store, sit on a chair, and if it were comfortable and fit our budget, ask if they delivered because I have never enjoyed carrying large pieces of furniture. And furniture people are experts at carrying anyway.

If they did deliver, I would place the order and leave. If they did not, I would leave without the chair after expressing a suitable amount of indignation. Any furniture store that does not offer free delivery or does not deliver at all does not deserve to stay in business. One especially interesting facet of furniture shopping is that the furniture you order never looks that good after they deliver it to your house.

"Is that what we ordered?" you will ask the delivery guy, sure a mistake has been made. He will smile as he hands you the delivery slip because he has heard that statement many times. And my wife would be as likely to let me shop alone for furniture as I would be to ask her to run to the hardware store and get a good power drill. Even in our earlier marital years, we did not have a treaty provision that covered furniture shopping. It was a serious omission, as I would discover. Let me relate one sad story about our furniture shopping.

Our Asheville home buyer wanted most of the furniture. I suspect that the husband felt he had dodged a bullet by buying everything in our house and probably laughed at what was waiting in the furniture stores, but for me, not him, and I still curse his memory. Some of my experiences as we returned to furniture shopping are heart-wrenching for me to describe. Although I don't think I have ever had my heart wrenched. Not yet, anyway.

This particular event, "the chair episode," turned out to be a two-week event. I will list the various components in order, although the time frame for each event varied. And remember, this is just one chair! At the time, in preparation for our move to The Home, we had yet to shop for a couch, a bedroom set, a dining room table, and more. All those shopping trips are now a mental blur, and that is probably a good thing.

1. Mery decides we need a new chair. "That one in front of the fireplace never looked right, and I'd like to have a new chair before we move." And so we (i.e., I) carried the old chair into the garage, where it sat for several weeks. We contacted two charities and a neighbor who could have used a chair; if you went to his house, there was never a comfortable place to sit.

But I was amazed; no one, even the neighbor, wanted our beautiful chair. When we first got married, no one threw away nice chairs. Any chairs sitting on curbs waiting for the garbage pickup looked as though they had been used by a mother dog and her litter of puppies. If anyone put a nice chair out on the curb, people would be fighting over it. But no one fought over our chair. How the times have changed! We eventually took the chair to the Children's Home resale store. For all I know, it might still be there.

2. We go shopping; Mery finally selected a chair at Rooms To Go. This was our fifth store that day, and at this point, I would have purchased a chair carved from some insect-infested tree. And I don't know why they call their stores "Rooms to Go" because when we purchased the chair, it had to be ordered.

3. The new chair was delivered, and I loved it. It was one of the most comfortable chairs I have ever had. But my feelings were not important. "That chair doesn't fit the room," Mery insisted. "It is much too large." Despite my tears—I may have even promised she could purchase an outside statue—the chair had to go. We were still operating according to the tenets of our marital treaty! But that treaty was already close to obsolete. Very soon, it would be null and void. I mean, null!

4. We made another trip to the store and selected another chair—fortunately, one that was ready to go, and the substitute arrived several days later. The new chair was comfortable, not as much as the other chair, but still one that most people, including me, would regard as a nice place to sit. But what we thought was a recliner was not. I had no problem with the absence of this feature, and I was apprehensive about returning to the store with a dubious claim that the store made a serious error, giving us what we thought was a recliner but was not.

We trudged back to the store. The store manager was doubtful about our claim of their negligence, but he agreed on another switch with no additional delivery charges. But as we left, I thought I saw a picture of Mery on the employee bulletin board, with the written notation, in large red letters, "If this person enters the store, contact the manager immediately."

Maybe we had been placed on his list of "difficult customers." I wonder if furniture stores had computerized lists of difficult customers and sent the lists via closed email circuits to other furniture stores. If so, we might have been in trouble during our subsequent shopping visits. But being on a "furniture purchase watch" list would not have bothered me.

5. The next chair arrived. It was comfortable, and I decided that the episode was finished. But a few weeks later, I discovered that it was not finished. Mery wanted me to saw the legs off of the chair so "our shorter friends can sit there and have their feet touch the ground." I told her that it would be easier if she just got taller friends, that there were probably hundreds of tall people out there, and it made no sense to saw off chair legs. She was not convinced.

Fortunately, this leg-sawing never took place. But if you are thinking that at least they had one new piece of furniture for their new home, you would be wrong. The couple who bought our house bought pretty much all our furniture. Even that new chair! So we saved no shopping time. The personal agony involved with that chair was for naught, and I had to do it again.

When I am in the furniture shopping arena with Mery, there is no endpoint to the process. Sometimes I feel as though I am living in that old *Flash Gordon* series, where one session ends with Prince Baron falling into a pit of lava, you are horrified and depressed because Prince Baron was a good guy and you liked him, but then next week, you find out that the Prince had picked up a long rope thrown from a passing spaceship by Flash Gordon, who had just finished his dinner date with Aura, Ming's daughter, and was on his way home.

The special effects of that old television series were not great even then and would be considered pathetic today. I guess that is the reason we don't see any reruns. But when I was a kid, I didn't miss an episode. You never knew when Flash might be a little late, maybe lingering too long over dinner, and the Clay People would capture Dale and do who knows what to her. The Clay People were incredibly sinister. And if you don't remember what the Clay People looked like, it is too bad. But you might be able to stream the series.

I lived this furniture nightmare for weeks, driving in heavy traffic, sometimes in the rain, from one large furniture store to the next, purchasing items and ignoring others, and then, to the salesperson's consternation, when we bought something, Mery asked that they put the item on layaway. As part of my moving back into the furniture shopping world, I discovered that furniture stores don't love "layaways." They usually offer the service, but reluctantly. I think it is fair to say that most furniture stores hate layaways. Layaways are like "incompletes" in a university course. You are delaying an outcome, and that delay never bodes well for anyone.

Furniture stores like to sell an item, deliver it, and then remove it from their inventory. Storing it in their closet or warehouse is not an attractive prospect, and I can't blame them. Changed minds or altered plans can happen during a layaway. But the stores do it because they often impose a significant penalty for canceled layaway, on the order of, "you lose the purchase price and pay a twenty-five percent penalty on top of that. We also take possession of your car."

During our excursions, we (i.e., Mery) might find a nice couch, but she didn't think it went with the chair we had on layaway. "Let's go see if we can get the chair in a different color. And maybe a different style because I don't want a swivel chair now because it won't work with the table I want to get." You can imagine the furniture people's faces when we reappear in the store and ask them to alter the nature of our earlier layaway. Her picture probably ended up on more bulletin boards.

During these sojourns, Mery took an incredible number of pictures with her phone and pulled the pictures up as she shopped for matching items. I don't know how many pictures she accumulated, and I don't want to know. Did Steve Jobs know what he was doing when he installed cameras on iPhones? He might be laughing now about all the misery he produced—if he is in a place where he can laugh.

Our pending move created another issue: how to allocate the limited space we were going to inhabit. The existing treaty was null, and we would have to renegotiate, But I was entering this important dispute, this uncharted territory, without a weapon! If you kept up with all the issues involved in Brexit, I can assure you that their issues were a cakewalk compared to our move.

If you have ever seen *Ben-Hur*, I felt like the guy going into that tournament with a chariot pulled by four little ponies. I am in line, looking over at my competitor, a sinister man with four large black Arabian stallions, and as if he needed more advantages, he had grinders on his chariot wheels, devices designed to shred not only your chariot but your ponies too. How is that fair?

That chariot race is a useful image when you visualize our discussions about using our new and limited personal space. In case you weren't sure, Mery is the one driving the chariot with the grinders. For the first time since we got married, I had no treaty rights and, even worse, nothing with which to negotiate a deal.

I could visualize Mery licking her lips at the idea of being able to arrange the entire household without worrying about what I would prefer. Personal space wasn't a problem at the new place because whenever Mery needed more, she took some of mine, since, as she explained, "You weren't using it anyway." But initially, probably because I was mentally exhausted from furniture shopping, I didn't care about personal space.

Mery had obtained the floor plans for our new apartment weeks before we moved. She seemed to find a way to do such things, and she proceeded to sketch her battle plans. It was really more of a skirmish than a battle because I had no idea what the hell I was doing. And when she said things like, "I'll need the big walk-in closet for my things," I didn't bat an eye. I don't remember ever batting just one of my eyes."

Walk-in closet? What the hell was that? I couldn't remember the last time I ever walked into a closet. I never knew you could. I would reach into that dark, cluttered room, grab a shirt or pants, and shut the door. We never had a walk-in closet before. I saw them in the houses of friends but not in any of ours. I had some hard lessons coming about limited space.

Generalizations should be tenuous, but I would argue that adjustments to reduced living spaces are more difficult for males. Even without the kind of treaty Mery and I had, husbands generally focused their limited attention spans on their outside worlds, places where they could crawl and dig and plant. Their yards may have been small, but they were places they could ride around like lords of the manor. Instead of a horse, they might be sitting on a John Deer mower with a cart to hold their weapons.

I remember once, years ago, debating the relative merits of tractors with my neighbor. We finally decided that the only way to settle the question of which tractor was the more powerful was to conduct a test. Such ideas seem better after a few beers.

We got a long chain, attached it to the backs of the respective tractors, his John Deere and my Toro, and commenced to pulling. We'd both be at full throttle, and all eight tractor wheels would be churning gravel. Neither of us was moving, but neither of us was giving up! One of us would shift into neutral, back up, and hit the throttle again, trying for momentum to pull our opponent over the line. But the power contest pretty much stayed a draw until the chain finally broke. All in all, it was a fun afternoon.

But like the Flash Gordon adventures, with hot lava pools and Dale Arden tied up in Emperor Ming's bedroom, all my backyard adventures are just pleasant memories. I am no longer driving a tractor or owning any yard implements. Now we are squabbling over what were once territorial crumbs.

When we moved into the new apartment, Mery hung one of those shoe trees on the closet door of the storage room she had allocated to me. I thought, at the time, this would be plenty of room for the few shoes I had. And that will give you some idea of where I was, now thinking about spaces for my shoes instead of where I would put my new chain saw!

I think it was about a week later that I noticed several pairs of her shoes hanging on what I thought was my shoe tree. When I mentioned it, she said, "You don't have that many shoes anyway, and I needed the space." As I write this, three of the five shelves on my tree have her shoes.

It might also be appropriate to note that most of the other shelving in "my" closet contains our spare sheets and blankets. I apparently "didn't need those shelves either!" And though I might agree that I didn't need them *right now*, it would have been nice to have room to expand in case I bought a chainsaw. I had forgotten the bargains you can get on a chainsaw in February. I think I miss going to Ace Hardware the most. Those stores are staffed with people who know all sorts of fascinating things about what is going on in your house, and I rarely went a week without stopping to chat and buy. Ace is easily my favorite store.

All the memories are only poignant thoughts about my previous life. We have no more treaties now because negotiating a treaty implies bargaining power on both sides. I have no power now, and everyone knows this. Mery certainly knows it. I am like the hapless tenant in the corner unit of a large apartment building who is waiting for the landlord's next command that he will have to move again because they need his unit to expand the kitchen of the adjoining unit, but I shouldn't worry because there is a nice apartment in the basement. Or it will be nice after the owner gets rid of the old furnace and cleans the place up a bit.

But life goes on. You adjust to the changes, and yesterday's nightmare becomes today's lifestyle. You adjust, or you die.

Dave:

Before providing more details, far more than you wanted, about "The Home," I want to pay my respects to your "conception card" to Mery. It was an insightful and thought-provoking card, one that brought a smile even to Mery's tired face. And it saddened me to realize yet again that our "Conception Day" concept has not caught on. But it ain't over yet!

We are still unpacking, and the hard labor is taking a toll on both of us. Mostly on Mery. She hurt her knee (naturally, I was responsible because I left a piece of plastic sheeting on the floor where she could trip on it), and she is now shopping for a walker. When I was taking her to a therapy appointment, she was leaning on me, and we were walking very slowly to the car. I started laughing and told her that if anyone was watching, and someone was probably watching because there are windows everywhere here, they would be lamenting the "poor old people who have trouble walking."

We were on the way back from Salisbury yesterday, and I wasn't paying much attention to Mery as she was making a phone call to straighten out a "bad charge on her PayPal account." But when she started giving out information to this guy on the phone and downloaded a program to search out the presumably bad charges, I almost drove off the road.

To make a long story short, and I suppose it is too late for that, anyway, when we got home, I deleted the program and all traces of that phone call. I think we dodged a bullet there. More evidence for the warning that "You can't be too careful." Do you think you could be "too careful," Dave? Let me know.

This afternoon, while Mery was napping, I took a bottle of wine and sat on our new spacious porch, large enough for two chairs, a fake plant, me, and a bottle of wine. At Mery's behest, and believe me, Dave, she has a powerful behest, I downloaded the home's software for residents. I looked over the week's activities, and one of them involves a men's group that meets "just to talk and discuss items of interest."

From your vast experience, is being a guy enough raw material for a meeting, Dave? Or for a discussion? When Mery said that it sounded good to her, I realized how far apart we are in our current perspectives. The only rationale I can think of for such a group, I said to myself, because I often speak with myself, is that this weekly meeting involves guys who never had a chance to talk at home. Maybe not even at work! I can visualize the men sitting around a circle in a room with no windows or pictures on the walls, and they are staring at one another.

One guy, obviously the elected chair, gavels the meeting to order. No one seems to be taking notes.

"Well, the meeting is open for discussion. Who has a topic they want to bring up?"

Silence.

"Well, then, is there any old business? Anyone read any good books? Interesting articles in the paper? Do any of you still get a daily paper?"

More silence, even more pronounced.

One guy in the back (there are only five guys in attendance, and two of them are asleep) raises his hand. "I move we adjourn." No one votes, even the guy who made the motion.

The gavel comes down. "Motion carries. And we'll see you all next week for our semiannual potluck. Who wants to bring the beer?"

Much laughter as everyone files out. One of the

guys remains in his chair, still asleep and apparently having some sort of erotic dream.

Keep me in your thoughts and prayers.

Dan

6.

The New Neighbors!

Have you ever moved to the other side of your town or even to an entirely new city, searching for that elusive better life? Or maybe just for a cheaper house? Most Americans move at some point. If people had a "stay close to home" tendency, humankind might still be concentrated in Africa. That concentration would have been good for the planet, but maybe not so good for the elephants.

One of the first questions popping into your already harried mind as you survey the new surroundings is, "What are the neighbors like?" You hope, and maybe pray, even if praying is not your normal pattern, that your new neighbors will be nice. Maybe not nice enough that you want to have weekly barbeques in your backyards or spend evenings looking at one another's photo albums, but nice enough to at least smile at them as you mow your lawn or get your mail.

The routine chore of getting your mail could be a significant event during your first few days in the new neighborhood. You probably won't get anything important in the mail—very few of us do because everything seems to be done online now, and that is sad for us and the post office—but getting your mail has evolved from a legal event to a social one. That mailbox may be your major contact point for your neighborhood interactions. People's furniture deliveries will arrive on that street, as will their Amazon deliveries and maybe even their food. You will take your dog for walks on that street . . . if you have a dog.

Being on your street, even for a few minutes, provides an opportunity to meet your new neighbors. Because you probably won't have a front porch to sit on—few new homes now come with front porches. Americans are more involved with their backyards, the patches of ground with some privacy, where they can put up volleyball nets and plant gardens that seldom yield much in the way of fruits or vegetables. Except for zucchini. Everyone seems to harvest a good crop of zucchini. And that may or may not be a good thing, depending on how you feel about zucchini. I don't particularly like it, but it makes great bread.

Americans define "neighbor" in different ways. For example, you might say that your neighbor is the family next door, and most of us would go along with that. But does that definition mean both sides of your house? And what about two doors from you? Is that guy going to get an invitation to stop by your house for coffee? Or to look at your photo album?

The point is, where are you going to draw the neighbor line? Will your line extend to the end of the block? Suppose your house is already on the end of the block. That corner location means your next-door neighbor is across the street. What then? And we haven't even discussed the family across the street yet. Including them effectively doubles your number of neighbors. Where will it stop?

And the complex situation poses some interesting social problems. What happens if you don't see the people across the street as neighbors, but they see you as one?

In my younger years, our family always lived in Chicago apartments, and the only people we ever thought about as neighbors were the ones who lived in the same building. Anyone else, the people across the street, for example, might as well be in another city. My wife still finds it difficult to believe that we lived in one neighborhood for ten years and never met anyone across the street or even next door to the apartment building. I don't think we ever laid eyes on any of these people, and when we left that neighborhood for good, I doubt any of the potential neighbors even noticed we were gone.

After you meet most of the neighbors—however you define that term—you might meet a few unpleasant people in the group. Unfortunately, there are unpleasant people in many neighborhoods, individuals who make life more difficult for the rest of us. Some of the more unpleasant ones seem to run for public office. And there is another interesting research question.

You will probably be able to avoid regular contact with unpleasant politicians, but bad neighbors might be yours to deal with for a long time. What exactly is a "bad neighbor"? The answer depends on who you ask. I remember listening to my relatives talk about their neighbors, easily their favorite pastime. One uncle didn't like his neighbor because "the guy talks with an accent."

The people in that neighborhood probably had meetings about how best to deal with my uncle.

Another uncle didn't like a neighbor because "the guy spends too much time in his yard." What difference did that activity make to my uncle? It may have made him feel guilty because I never saw this uncle with a rake in his hand. In a few years, that uncle could have been talking about me when he complained about a neighbor working all day in the yard.

I don't remember any of my relatives having even a cursory friendship with a neighbor. Individuals in my family generally regarded their neighbors as potential threats to their safety and well-being. Their strategy was to keep people they didn't know or trust as far away from them as possible. I don't think that it would have been difficult for them to accomplish that goal because none of my relatives were the warm and fuzzy types. It would have been interesting to hear the over-the-fence discussions that their neighbors had about my family.

Fortunately, my wife and I had different experiences. Overall, we had very positive neighbor relationships. In all of our many moves, we hoped and expected that our neighbors would be good people. Considering we moved more than twelve times during our marriage, we had a lot of experience meeting new people. When we moved to Michigan, our newest next-door neighbor brought over her homemade brownies. She wanted to welcome us to the neighborhood. Months later, she dropped by and wondered if we liked her brownies or if something had been wrong with them because we never said anything. Apparently, people always raved about them. Or so she said.

I didn't buy into the "Oh, by the way . . ." approach she used when she asked about the brownies; I think she was irritated that we didn't say anything. Brownies were her keystone dish, and she was accustomed to recipients gushing over them. I'm guessing that her husband finally told her to "go next door and ask them if they liked your damn brownies."

Therein lies an interesting tale about an event that could have gone in various directions, each of which would have changed the course of our lives. Well, not really. But things could have turned out differently in the neighborhood because of what happened to the brownies. When she brought them to our door, I put the brownies on the kitchen counter because we were busy unpacking. I thanked her and told her we couldn't wait to eat them. That was an exaggeration because I could live the rest of my life without eating another brownie. Too rich for my taste.

I am surprised that I forgot about our golden retriever, Jake, because we always had to watch that dog. He poked his nose into almost anything, anywhere in the house, and he had no scruples when it came to the household food supply. And for him, most things had the potential of being food. He was willing to try anything. Jake had eaten more than one sock.

Anyway, Jake devoured all the brownies while we were busy with other things. He never got sick, so it was just one more episode of Jake being a bad dog. We didn't mention the neighbor's brownies or compliment her because we had no idea how they tasted. We couldn't lie. Well, I could have. I come from a long line of people who stretch the truth far beyond what most people would consider reasonable, and I learned from them.

But Mery is different. If she was telling a lie, and she knew it, she would look guilty; when Mery lies, she has an easy-to-read expression, red-faced, and considerable stammering when she talks. If the cops ever brought her in for an interrogation about a crime I committed, it would be over in minutes, and I would be headed to the slammer.

So it would be easy for even an amateur, like our new neighbor, to catch us in a lie. She could have said something outlandish like, "I was trying a new recipe from my Swedish relatives and thought I might have put too much kale in the brownies."

Mery's face would have turned red, and she would have stammered, "Oh, no, I have always loved kale." (She does not.) To avoid any interrogation and embarrassment, we just avoided brownie talk. She brought them on a paper plate, so there was nothing to be returned.

Two years later, we finally told her what happened to her brownies, and she took it well. She did not laugh, but she nodded and said, "I thought it might have been something like that." She and her husband turned out to be some of our best neighbors, but we never received another batch of her signature brownies.

Our first move to a house was in Elgin, Illinois, with the typical postage stamp-sized front lot and a one-car garage. If you were raking one side of your lawn, the end of your rake could have poked your neighbor in the eye if he was weeding. But the neighborhood seemed nice, with a mixture of ages and ethnic groups and a great place for biking and walking.

The lady across the street came over the first week and, after uttering the usual welcome, informed us that the previous owner would go out with tweezers to weed the front lawn every week. I told her she wouldn't be seeing me out there with tweezers. I said that we didn't even own any tweezers.

She took the news pretty well, but I don't remember seeing her again, and I noticed her front curtains moving when I mowed our front lawn. Overall, though, she was a nice neighbor. Sometimes the best neighbors are those you don't see very often.

That small house produced my first neighborly confrontation, and it involved property lines. In some cities, especially those with small lots, people can become protective of their properties. I think there is an interesting principle here: the smaller the lot, the more protective people are.

We had a front lawn that was about six inches on the neighbor's property. The bizarre boundary line was probably the result of land shifting or surveyor error; whatever the cause, it didn't matter, at least to me. But my neighbor was fixated on his property line, so when he mowed his lawn every week, rain or shine, he mowed that six-inch strip in front of our house.

I assured him that I knew where his property line was, but it looked a little silly for our front lawn to have a six-inch band with a different height than the rest. Our front lawn usually looked like a bad haircut. But I never could persuade him to just let me mow "his lawn," so the strange cutting process continued for the entire time we lived in that house. Other than that, he was a decent neighbor.

A few years later, we bought three acres of wooded land in Hampshire, Illinois, and built a log house. We had more land, but we also had drainage problems, so we planted a few hundred trees. One of our new neighbors complained, saying he had always driven his tractor over our land to get to his friend's house and wondered if we would object to his continuing the practice.

I explained that I would have a problem, that we had planted trees across his path, and he would have to find another way to his friend's house, one that was not going across our land. He did not take the refusal well. A few days later, "no trespassing" signs appeared on his trees facing our land. We never spoke again. It wasn't much of a problem since we both had ample acreage and woods, and we never came face-to-face. We left that community without saying any goodbyes to him.

If you have a bad neighbor, you feel as though you should say something to the people who buy your house, alerting the buyers to be careful. It is an interesting ethical question. Do you tell them before the sale, after, or not at all? After all, your bad neighbor could become the buyer's best friend. I'm sure things like that happen.

Conversely, if you have great neighbors, you could bump your price up a few thousand dollars before you sign the contracts. "Good neighbors are priceless," you could tell the potential buyers, and not many people would argue the point.

We had to remind ourselves each time we moved that we were a little worried about getting used to new neighbors, but so were the current residents. They are trying to size up the new arrival at the same time the arrival is sizing them up. When you move into a neighborhood, there is an established pattern of behavior forged through years of sometimes painful experiences. People know who has the power tools, who is willing to lend equipment, and who is available to help move a couch or cut down a tree. And now, here comes a new arrival. Everyone is on edge!

The most pleasant, stress-free move was to our first home in Asheville. One of the homeowners had a get-acquainted wine and cheese party to introduce everyone to us, and vice versa. It was like an employment interview, except that the job had been filled. By us. But it worked out well, and we felt comfortable from the first day, waving to everyone on the way to our mailbox.

And then came the retirement community. We didn't worry about established patterns because we were going to a new building. We would be the first to put furniture on the outside porch. We would be among the first to take garbage to the trash room—the "refuse recycling center," as it should be called. We would be getting used to the new mailroom just like the rest of them. We didn't have to worry about breaking rules or violating sensibilities. No one got upset with a new neighbor during the three-week period when everyone moved into the building because we were all new!

Our new home was an apartment located on the second floor in one of the four-story high-rises. It doesn't seem reasonable to describe a four-story building as a "high-rise." New Yorkers would laugh at me if I told them I lived in a high-rise. They would probably describe the apartment as a modified ranch house. A New Yorker would then explain that you could survive a fall from the fourth floor. A few of them might throw you off the roof to prove their point. New Yorkers are like that!

Drawing from the available research, the median lethal distance for a fall is forty-eight feet or four stories. Only about half of us could survive falling from a four-story building. All things considered, then, I still think it is fair to describe our new building as a high-rise, so the hell with what New Yorkers might say.

There are obvious advantages to high-rise living, and the pluses explain their continuing popularity. Builders and contractors prefer the structures because the economical use of space means that they can place more people in less area. It is also easier to provide utilities to residents when you have them in a confined area. You can also make more public space available for things like parks and parking lots if the residential structures go up rather than out.

But as usual, there is a downside. If the buildings are not well-constructed and properly insulated, the noise level between units can be a quality-of-life problem, not only for the individual residents but for the relationship between residents. Knocking on your ceiling to inform the resident upstairs that he is making too much noise does not encourage harmony. Neither does going next door to complain about television volume. Unfortunately, most building codes deal with safety, not comfort, sounds, or even visual appeal.

You can encounter cleanliness problems with a building's public spaces. New residents may have different perspectives on their responsibilities for the common areas. When an area belongs to everyone, like the garbage room, mailroom, and lobby, it belongs to no one. When I yelled at a lady once for dumping her car's ashtray into a shopping mall parking lot, she yelled right back, "Butt out. This parking lot doesn't belong to you!" I laughed at her unintended wordplay, but not her attitude.

That woman in the mall lot might have been sloppy and inconsiderate, but she was correct. Public spaces belong to everyone and not to any single individual. This is an underlying reason why public areas can deteriorate if they are not properly and regularly maintained. The garbage mounds in the nation's national and state parks attest to this persistent problem. Fortunately, we didn't face this situation in our building, probably because of the persistent efforts of a conscientious maintenance crew.

One issue that did emerge was a common one with high-rise residents. People living in high-rise structures often complain that they "never get to know anyone." Such complaints are due to the nature of the buildings. It is harder to meet your neighbors when you live in a high-rise. Hallways are carpeted paths to the comfort and safety of your apartment. But they are also a virtual no-man's-land, places where people hesitate to venture because they don't feel comfortable. I discussed this situation earlier.

I lived in a building in Oak Park, Illinois, for a year and never made contact with another resident. One morning, I saw a note on the building's lobby door: "I've lived here for six months and haven't met anyone in this building. I'm having a wine and cheese party on Friday night, and I hope you will stop by to get acquainted." His invitation sounded appealing. But the next day, in big red letters, he had written on his earlier note, "Never mind! I canceled the party." I never found out why, and I never met the guy to ask.

With the research results swirling around my cluttered mind, I had a few concerns about moving to a high-rise. On the other hand, this was a retirement community. And there was an established structure for the dissemination of information. Our building was organized into clusters, with most building floors constituting a cluster. The clusters met periodically, sometimes monthly, but it was up to each group how often they met. But as a result, gradually and inevitably, the residents got acquainted. It was possible to greet people by name rather than just nodding as you passed one another in those hallways. The familiarity created a more comfortable environment, but it was still rare to meet residents in the hallway.

The residents here are also older than in other high-rise communities. When we moved in, the average age was in the upper seventies. We knew that we would probably not have to worry about our neighbor's late-night parties. We attended a fundraising event in the community room one evening, and the moderator commented, "I know it's getting late, so we'll try to wrap this up." It was eight o'clock.

The residents here also come from higher income brackets, which was not surprising, given the high entrance fee. When I looked through the directory, I saw retired physicians, surgeons, lawyers, dentists, CEOs, and teachers; this higher educational and professional spectrum probably meant a more tolerant and inclusive social environment. During the first few months, I saw and heard nothing to dispute that conclusion. If you have the money and resources to move here, you are going to be welcome.

One of the more personally difficult things about moving to a retirement community is the question of attitudes. The residents here were apparently successful during their working lives, but they are no longer what they were. They spent their adult lives working in a profession and achieved varying degrees of success and recognition. Some of them, according to their profiles, were very successful.

But things change after retirement. Some residents might have been successful trial lawyers, but not now. Individuals may occupy their leisure time making birdhouses. Some residents had successful careers as psychologists and therapists, writing books, giving lectures, and advising clients, but now they spend time on resident committees that evaluate meal preparation.

Such dramatic personal changes after retirement are not unique to this community. They are usually inevitable and a major reason why many Americans are apprehensive about their retirements. We hear about these feelings and apprehensions in arenas from politics to sports. People worry about their retirements; "I don't know what I'm going to do. This is all I have ever done. This is who I am."

One of our friends was a college dean and an expert in outdoor education. He dreaded retirement because it was difficult for him to imagine the resulting change in his life. And in how people would react to him. Another friend, a physician, worked hard to get through medical school and enjoyed being "a doctor." He is getting close to eighty years old and hasn't retired yet.

I was surprised that I hadn't seen much of this frustration. I have noticed a few residents who are still working part-time in their professions, but most are busy with other things, like the placement of planter boxes. And they give every indication that they are throwing themselves into their new projects. I think that residents here have already adjusted to their retirements and that their initial traumas, if there were any, are over. They moved to this community after passing through their most difficult adjustment periods.

I have had conversations with a few residents about a wide variety of topics, ranging from the upcoming elections—and lately, it seems as though there is always an "upcoming election"—to the quality of the last meal, and I usually ask what their previous careers were. It is interesting not because of what those careers were, but that I had to ask. Most residents here seem to have successfully redefined themselves.

So, who do we have for our new neighbors? I would categorize them as a group of successful, energetic, and friendly individuals who are trying to establish appealing and rewarding activities for this final segment of their lives. And they seem to be doing well at it.

Maybe a good way to summarize this last move of ours is that we landed in a good neighborhood. And that is a comfortable feeling.

Dave:

    Do you ever take a few minutes to look at the types of people you enjoy hanging with? Who are your friends, Dave? Is there much difference in their ages, educations, and ethnicities, or are they pretty much mirrors of you? Do you enjoy, and I mean really enjoy, the time you spend with these people? Are they your close *friends*, whatever that ambiguous term means?

    I'm going to lay out a couple of details about my friendship pattern, Dave, and it involves you, so please pay more attention than you customarily do to my emails. Anyway, it seems that my friendship picture is a little weird. I don't know how or why it happened. Mery noticed and mentioned it when I told her that I should call Dave (meaning you!), and she said, "Which Dave? Do you know how many guys you hang out with who are Daves?"

    I didn't know! Or I never thought much about it. But her comment started me thinking about not only my friends but also friendships in general.

    Anyway, the first, and maybe most important, point here is that I don't select my friends by their names. At least, I didn't think I did. Who would begin a friend search by looking for someone with a specific name? And how many people search for more friends anyway?

    I think we acquire our friends by accident. I don't know about you, but I know I do! For example, a new relationship might start at the local gym. You meet someone running on the adjoining treadmill, you start talking, share a few laughs about the equipment or your exercise plans, and decide that there is something about him or her that you like.

    Maybe it was something simple at first, like their laugh. A person's laugh has always been a factor in deciding how I feel about them. I like people who have a good laugh. President Obama has a good laugh; Donald Trump does not. After you realize that you like listening to this person's stories, or laughs, you might have a new friend. Or you might not. And these new friends can go off your network faster than they came onto it, so hanging on to your friendships can be challenging. By the way, I have always liked your laugh, Dave.

A few people, not many, maintain their school friendships, and I suppose hanging on is psychologically easier than cutting adolescent ties. Whenever I ask about their school friendships, people will shrug and admit that if they met those same individuals today, they would not be friends.

Let's get back to my Dave list. I didn't know any of you in school! In your case, you are obviously the husband of my wife's friend, if you can follow that jagged connection. Our friendship started from our spouse's relationship and grew because you and I had similar critical perspectives on the world. And we were both bad golfers. Bad golf and social cynicism were more than enough to nurture our friendship.

And the other Daves? Another was a university colleague. We started having coffee before classes. I like coffee, and I like people who like coffee. I developed a great chemistry with this guy. It wasn't his coffee because that Dave made terrible coffee; he probably still does.

My friendships with you guys always took time to develop. I don't think the two of us developed instant chemistry, and this longer time frame seems more common for males. I always need time, sometimes a lot, before considering someone a friend, but Mery can make a friend during an elevator ride. In fairness to her, the ride would have to involve at least three stops. If that sounds like an exaggeration, I remember sitting in our living room, listening to a thirty-minute telephone conversation she had with some guy after answering his *misdial*.

The nature of friendships is shifting in today's world, and in my mind, not in a positive direction. I remember a classroom lecture I gave on friendship and relationships. When I emphasized that personal contact was essential, I could see heads shaking around the room. One student told me that he had more than fifty "good friends," and "I've never met any of them face-to-face."

Time changes things, and the definition of a close friendship has shifted in recent years. People, especially younger people, move around a lot now, and they often don't have the time or inclination to nurture friendships with regular personal contact. They use their computers and iPhones for updates on current events, job applications, dating, and apparently making and keeping their friends. But I don't think their electronic and transient friendships are good over the long term.

Back to the Dave pattern! Other than their first names, my friends don't have much in common. Dave W—bad coffee guy—is a physicist with quirks, even for a physicist. And there is you, a special education teacher with a razor wit and incredible carpentry skills. You built a playhouse for your cats that could have made it into *Architectural Digest* if it ever decided to feature cathouses. I enjoy playing golf with you because we play at the same skill level that is often described, not in a kind way, as duffer golf.

Mery once suggested, "You should get all your Dave friends together, maybe with a Zoom call. It would be fascinating, and I'd be glad to help you set it up." She Zooms with her various networks on a regular basis and seems to enjoy it. I have yet to do my first.

Getting my friends together, Zooming or otherwise, is not a good idea. There are sociometric principles involved. If you ignore them, you face the prospect of major disappointments. For example, because Allen likes Dave and also Charlie, Allen should not assume that Dave would like Charlie. It is possible that Dave and Charlie will hate one another, argue about controversial politics or golf, and start a fistfight, maybe resulting in serious injuries to Charlie. And then what is Allen going to do? Social relationships are not like algebraic equations, Dave.

Hard to believe, there are more Daves on my list, but no pattern there either. Mery tried to suggest that the Daves could be *doppelgängers*, but that silly notion doesn't stand up under even casual scrutiny.

If you are unfamiliar with the term, a doppelgänger is more like your behavioral twin. This individual may or may not look like you, but they might resemble the way you walk or dress. Or maybe have the same favorite restaurants. No one knows where your doppelgänger comes from, and few people think much about the idea. Maybe our distant ancestors hooked up for a casual encounter on the boat coming to New York, and we share DNA with these apparent strangers. But you and the other Daves do not share many of my habits, so I can forget that explanation.

Maybe there were just more guys with that name years ago. If the name "David" were popular when I was born, it would be logical to have more Daves as friends. But I checked, and "David" was fifth or sixth through the 1940s and '50s. David never hit number one or number two. It has to make you wonder, *What's not to like about "David?"* Your parents obviously liked the name.

After all this pondering with no answers, I was back to my initial question. Is there an underlying dynamic with my friendships? Maybe I have an unconscious name fetish! If I met a friendly person at the gym named Ernie, could that turn into a close friendship? Would I envelop Ernie in the warmth of my personal network or brush him off like a seasonal pest, nodding as we threw our towels in the bin because he didn't have the right name?

What happens if I meet someone in that same gym whose behavior and attitude is offensive? The guy was a right-wing QAnon member, a religious zealot, and he hated coffee. But he had a great laugh and answered to "Dave!" Would this person become a close friend just because of his name?

What started as a casual investigation was more involved and interesting than I thought. I learned more about friendships, enough to convince me that despite our society's love for computers, technology is no substitute for personal contact. What are your friends worth? You may not ask until you are confronted with a difficult situation, when you need the comfort provided by someone you know and trust.

I hope you realize, Dave, that despite the impressive length of your Facebook friend list, your computer "friends" will not be at your front door to offer help when you need it. Americans don't understand this. A magazine article (and no, I'm not going to provide the citation!) pointed out that a surprising proportion of Americans listed "Siri" as a close friend. Full disclosure: as a second grader, one of my "friends" was an abandoned automobile tire.

But we can't acquire supportive relationships by

staring at a computer terminal, posting pictures on Facebook, or composing three-line tweets. The people we will rely on, the people we have to rely on, will be people we know and trust, talk to, listen to, laugh with, share a meal or coffee with, or play a round of bad golf with. Personal contact is what provides us with caring people who will be at our front door when we need support.

The other friends, those from Facebook or Peloton, will fade as fast as they appeared. Computer friendships are convenient, fun, and useful, but electronic relationships disappear when we shut off our computers. That trait is their unique strength and their unique weakness.

Sorry I went on so long. If I were in a room with a guy who started to unwind on an esoteric topic, I'd find a reason to leave. "I have to use the bathroom" is great for such matters, and I wouldn't come back until he was finished. No one is going to quiz you about the time you spent in the john.

I remember being at a party with a guy who lectured everyone about Marxism and its influence on contemporary politics. I think I asked him if there was going to be an exam afterward. Then I said I had to go to the bathroom. I haven't seen him since.

What about explaining the unusual number of my friends named Dave? After hours of reflection, Dave, I've decided that sometimes a cigar is just a cigar.

Keep in touch.

Dan

7.

What the Hell Happened?*

*This chapter is based on an earlier version in my book, *Golden Years My Ass*! Some topics warrant repeating, and the negative attitude about getting old is one of them.

> "Man, whose young passion sets the spindrift flying,
>
> Is soon too lame to march, too cold for loving."
>
> —John Masefield

> "I can't chew the leather anymore..."
>
> —from *Scent of a Woman*

Who is John Masefield, and why should we care what he said? Well, forget him. I am more concerned with another issue: what happens to us and to me as the years unfold? Call it an epiphany. That may not be the most accurate term, but I might not ever find the perfect words to describe the sudden realization that "My god, I'm getting older!" Or worse, "My god, I'm old!"

It may be a birthday, an event—like the twentieth wedding anniversary of a kid you used to babysit—or the funeral of a high school acquaintance. Sometimes, it's your reflection. You wonder if someone put a trick mirror in your bathroom—that reflection couldn't be you. Because you don't feel *that* old, not as old as you look. Not as old as the birthdays remind you.

However and whenever it happens, you will come to the uncomfortable realization that you are getting older. You might already be old! You never thought it would happen. It was stupid, thinking that the passage of time would operate differently for you. You may still think of yourself as that same person you always were, and maybe you are, at least a little. But the rest of the world has been moving and changing. You might be standing in the same spot, watching the parade, but standing still is no advantage, not when everyone and everything else is moving.

If you want to look, but maybe you shouldn't, the signs of getting older will be there. They will be small signals—your radio set to the golden oldies station because you can't get into the current music scene. You wonder what is wrong with "young people" with their focus on texting; "what is wrong with telephone calls?" you ask out loud, but no one is listening.

You might play golf now, something you never did when you were younger, but there will be pressures for you to play. People will be surprised if you don't play a few rounds every week because, as you have begun to understand, golf is an older person's pursuit. You don't have to join a league, although you will be encouraged to because it is the only way to ensure your morning tee times. But you will also have a dermatologist who advises you to "stay out of the sun."

You won't think about the dermatologist as you hack your way through nine holes once or twice a week and then head into a well-appointed clubhouse for a nice lunch, where you purchase more golf balls and shirts you don't need at the golf shop. Your lunchtime conversations will be peppered with medical terms like PSA, LDC, T3, T4, and TSA.

Getting older happens so damn fast. You couldn't wait to get out of high school, or many of us couldn't. If you are still going to high school reunions, I suppose you had a good time. But getting out of high school was mostly a good thing, a sign that we were finally on our way.

But then our lives went on this fast track that adults told us would happen. Their warnings didn't make sense to us. When you were a kid, you heard adults saying, "I haven't seen my friend Jim for ten years," and you thought, *How could anyone let ten years go by without seeing a good friend? I don't let a week go by without talking to my friends.* And now you are saying those same things, and the young people around you are rolling their eyes in amazement (if there are any young people around you).

Studies have shown that individuals incarcerated for more than twenty years report that their prison time passed by in a virtual flash. Most of us would guess that twenty years locked in prison would be excruciatingly slow. You would look out the window every evening, if you had a window, and stare at the wall calendar, marking off each day and waiting for the end of your sentence.

Why is growing old so sad? We all do it, and we know we are going to do it. But "knowing" you are going to get old doesn't mean you are going to glide into that final stage of your life. America is a youth-centered society—it has been almost since its beginning—and being old means you are thrown out of the mainstream. That is not a comfortable idea, being thrown out.

Americans worship youth and the things that go along with being young. Vibrant physical appearances, boundless energy, and active lifestyles are the hallmarks of youth, and Americans desire these commodities. Americans want to stay young. Products to help us "look and feel younger" are a regular part of media advertising. I have never seen any ads for products that will help us look older.

Some of us age gracefully, but the evidence for the opposite, for the persistent discomfort about getting older, is overwhelming. Years ago, a clinical psychologist told me that three-fourths of his practice involved dealing with his patients' problems with growing older.

People are sensitive about how they look and feel as they get older. They know how they felt about old people when they were young, and they are guessing, probably accurately, that the current generation of young people feels the same about them.

Americans become sensitive about any references to their ages, especially after they move past "middle age." Years ago, I asked the birthday girl at a party how it felt to be in advanced middle age. (She was thirty-seven!) Her angry reaction was "visceral." I'm not sure she ever forgave me, although I'm also not sure why I would need to be forgiven.

Any social scientist using survey research can attest to the special care needed when asking respondents their ages. No professional researcher ever asks a direct question about age. If you ask the question directly, you are asking for no response or for an incorrect one. Research studies want accurate data on respondents' ages, so scientists will phrase the age question in different ways, maybe asking for the birth year or asking respondents which age category they belong in. It is apparently easier to say you belong in the thirty-six to forty-five category than to "admit" that you are forty-one years old.

Americans are especially uncomfortable moving into the next decade. Going into their thirties has apparently been the most difficult transition, although the transition into each new decade seems hard. If you examine graphs of age groupings, you often find an inordinate number of people who are "twenty-nine" and relatively few who are "thirty." It levels out by the time people get to "thirty-three," when they are accustomed to being "in their thirties." And this pattern occurs in every decade.

Many years ago, when I was researching nursing homes, I asked one resident her age. My inexperience showed because I was still using the direct approach. "Seventy-eight," she told me. After she left, another resident told me, "Don't believe her! She is "eighty-three, but she doesn't like the idea of being in her eighties." Americans apparently never get immune to this age sensitivity.

Unfortunately, physical appearance is a big part of who we are and how others define us. We start our lives being judged by attractiveness. We know that cute babies get more attention from strangers and even from their own families. And as the cuter babies get older, their lives are easier, at least if they remain cute. People respond to attractive individuals. Have you ever wondered why all television and sports broadcasters are attractive? Networks put attractive people on the air because viewers like looking at attractive announcers!

A few years ago, my friend, Jim, returned to graduate school to start a new career writing for magazines. When he arrived for his first day of class, there was a major assembly; all five hundred journalism majors gathered for a welcome speech by the dean. After his speech, the dean instructed the broadcast majors to move to another room. Jim told me, "Somewhat over half of the students left the hall. After a few minutes, the rest of us started laughing because we realized that all the attractive people left."

Even with the realization that most of us do not and will never have movie-star looks, we want to make the most of what we have. And keep what we have for as long as we can. We are going to dole out our money for lotions that will give us smooth skin, we are going to eat food that tastes like gauze so our digestive systems will operate more smoothly, and we will spend large amounts of money on unnecessary surgeries to improve our changing appearances. In our spare time, we will trudge to gyms and work with personal trainers to mold us into body shapes we never had, all part of the hopeless fight against the declines brought about by the advancing years. We will yank out the hairs growing where they don't belong, and we will try getting hair to grow in places it seems to have disappeared. All these desperate battles can be humorous, but they are also sad. Because the battles against advancing are hopeless. We are going to lose.

As if the physical changes aren't enough, there is also our diminished relevance as we get older, especially after retirement. You can see examples during sports interviews. When a former player interviews a current player, you can almost see the younger person thinking, *Yeah, like you even know what it is like to play now!*

Whenever I encounter someone teaching a university class, I

have this strong impulse to suggest something, maybe a great idea for presenting a difficult concept, but I usually stop myself. First, I know that the nature of university classrooms has changed. I never had to contend with students bringing their computers into the classroom and running a Google check on everything I said.

But younger teachers don't want to know what you think or how you did something because it's no longer "relevant." The presumed *wisdom of age* doesn't mean as much as it might have a generation ago.

I wrote my nephew a long letter a few months ago about applying for a job in the computer field. I was not a computer scientist, but we had a computer major at my university, so I had some understanding of trends in that field. I told my nephew that the field changes so fast that he can't possibly keep up while he waits for the right job. And he is probably being trained by instructors who are also not on the inside. His instructors are giving him useful but maybe obsolete knowledge. Jump into the job market now, I advised him, and start working in your field. He explained that I didn't understand how things are now, and he was dealing with his job situation in the best possible way. And he may have been right.

Growing older in this country is a challenge. Those of us in the latter stages of the life cycle can attest to its inherent difficulties. The physical and psychological assaults on our lives and sensibilities are fairly constant and hard to manage. But most of us do. Most of the time.

I have found it easier to deal with all the age-related assaults because of living in a retirement community. Everyone is older, so there is no reason to be stigmatized or traumatized by that insidious process. During dinner with a neighbor, she mentioned that, with all the problems she and her husband had, they felt comfortable because so many residents in the community had similar problems. The residents here are in the same aging boats, older people drifting on a turbulent sea of irrelevance and physical change, increasingly aware of that distant port, the place where boats will come into dock for the last time.

I apologize for the nautical metaphors, but I just finished watching *The Hunt for Red October*. I don't know what it is about water movies, but I love them, and I always have. Maybe growing up in Chicago, a city on Lake Michigan, had something to do with my water fetish. *The Sea Hawk* and *Captain Blood*, both with Errol Flynn, are two of the classic sea movies that, as my wife will attest, I never tire of watching. I especially love the line in *Captain Blood*, uttered during an emotional scene where the captain shoves one of his officers and says something like, *confound you, Jeremy, can't you just obey orders?*

What a great scene! People don't say, "confound you" anymore, and that's too bad. It is a wonderfully emotional expression of frustration. Anyway, I also never miss any of the WWII movies featuring destroyers and carriers headed out to sea to confront the enemy. My favorite television serial remains *Victory at Sea*. I don't know why I didn't go into the navy instead of the army.

Anyway, I guess John Masefield knew what he was talking about. Maybe it does happen too soon. I just wish I knew what a spindrift was.

Dave:

I have no doubt that you sat in your living room this past week and said, "I hope the Krauses are having a whale of a time on their cruise." And if you haven't given us a brief thought, well damn your hide! Haven't you heard about how good it is to send out "positive energy"?

Anyway, our trip was frustrating, agonizing, debilitating, and sometimes even painful. And that was on the good days. Let me skim through the major events for you, although it might be something like Meriwether Lewis writing in his diary . . . "kind of hot today, and met this Indian girl who is also hot. Ha ha."

Do you think that guy even had a sense of humor? And parenthetically, Dave, would you have named a son Meriwether? How on earth did he make it through high school with that name? Where was I?

Oh, yes, the trip. Well, I came down with the Green Apple Quick Step before leaving for the trip, so the PA suggested I ingest large amounts of Imodium coupled with regular bites from a Metamucil wafer. The two medicines seemed to work, but then we both came down with serious colds. I tried telling Mery that maybe this was the universe's way of telling us not to go. (Like many of our politicians, I am not averse to using theology when it helps my cause.) Unfortunately, she did not buy into the idea, and off to the rivers of Europe we went. Well, one river.

And our colds not only remained, they got progressively worse. We were hacking constantly, to the point where people on the boat did not want to sit with us in the dining room. I don't blame them. I didn't want to sit with us.

We ended up not going on a number of side trips

(e.g., come see how cheese is made; look inside a magnificent church that took 600 years to build, etc.) because we felt so lousy. My handkerchief looked as though I was wiping up mustard stains at Wrigley Field while eating one of their expensive and vile-tasting hot dogs. Does this image make you uncomfortable, Dave? Well, imagine how I felt, especially after I ran out of clean handkerchiefs and had to recycle them after they dried. You do some strange things when you travel, Dave. You adjust to your conditions. You adjust, or you die!

Interspersed with our personal conditions—and by the way, by this time, the Green Apple problem had resurfaced—you can add the tour director's explanation about "the worst weather we have ever had this late in March. I don't know what happened." I know what happened. It was cold.

And there was also the requirement to pass through various airport security checks that were tiring, unbelievably repetitive, and personally debilitating. (Have I already used that word?) Well, excuse me, but I don't give a shit.

Did anything good come from this trip, you might be asking? The answer is, one good thing! As we straggled out of that last airplane, I headed to the airport toilet with the speed of Donald Trump going to a beauty pageant. I told Mery not to mention airline travel for at least four years and never mention a river cruise. "Don't worry," she said. "I have no intention of going on another one of these either." But as you know, Mery's travel vows are seldom as permanent as mine.

And thus endeth our cruise experience. Our cruise director could have subbed for Buffalo Bob on *Howdy Doody*—do you remember Buffalo Bob and how bubbly he was? At the beginning of every show, he yelled, "Say, kids, what time is it" "And did you know what time it was, Dave? And did you shout it out with the rest of the kids in the room? Well, I'm going to tell you so you don't lose any sleep tonight. The answer you were supposed to yell, was "It's *Howdy Doody* time. It's time to start the show, so kids let's go." Ah, those were fun times.

Back to that tour director. Anyway, he had that kind of personality that, if you were in a good mood, was comforting. If not, and I definitely was not, you wanted to throttle him with the boat's anchor chain. And on the last night, with a stiff drink in his hand, because by that time, with all the cold weather, he probably needed one, he toasted the crowd (he had just finished explaining the boat's tipping policy) and said, with a small tear in his eye, "Be sad that it is all over, but smile at the memories you will always have."

What a bunch of shit! And I hope you forgive the persistent fecal analogy, but that is what is on my mind now. Well, as they say in Ireland, *May the wind be always at your back. May the sun shine warm upon your face, The rain fall soft upon your fields.*

Nice sentiment. Maybe I should be a tour director!
Dan

8.

Water Crisis at the Home!

"Water, water everywhere, nor any drop to drink." Those familiar words are from Samuel Taylor Coleridge's classic poem that American students had to learn—and hate—during their unpopular and unwanted high school English classes. In fairness to all the abused English teachers, how could they persuade students that this classic poem was relevant to them, that water was vital, that Coleridge had an important message, and they might face their own water crisis someday?

I think it was Winston Churchill who suggested, "Never let a good crisis go to waste." Has anyone thought about how British politicians seem more quotable than ours? But at least our elected representatives provide material for late-night comics. I suppose that is the trade-off. Maybe our next generation of politicians will be better. *Hope springs eternal!* By the way, that provocative quote comes from Alexander Pope, another English poet!

Anyway, just a few months after we arrived in our retirement community, a major problem emerged with the water supply. Or rather, the lack of it. The community didn't have water for more than a week, although it seemed longer. Time drags when you can't take a shower or wash your hands. If you were selecting essentials you would have a hard time doing without, would water be at the top of your list? Well, it should be!

If your furnace goes out, you can wear a sweater. If you are lucky enough to have a fireplace, you will have that possibility for heat. Fireplaces are not environmentally friendly, but they provide warmth, and when you are cold, environmental issues, unfortunately, take a backseat. If I were cold, I would throw our furniture, photo albums, and Consumer Reports into a fire with no guilt. Well, maybe a little.

And if the power goes out, you can light a few candles. And if you have a gas stove, you also have the prospect of a hot meal. So doing without heat or power is difficult but not impossible. For many, the hardest thing would be doing without their computers.

But no water? What can you do when you turn on the tap and you have nothing? I don't remember a time when there was no water in our Chicago apartment. My parents seemed to be constantly banging on our radiators for more heat during winter, and I never understood who was supposed to be hearing their banging. Anyway, we always had water in Chicago.

We lost power a lot when we lived in Hampshire, Illinois, and since we had a well, no power meant no water from the well pump. When there was going to be a *major storm*—it didn't take much for the electric company to classify a weather system as a major storm—it was a good bet that we would lose power. So we always filled one bathtub with water. Unless the power outage lasted more than a few days, we could at least flush our toilets.

If I listed my personal needs during a crisis, number one—or maybe number two, and I am not playing with words here—would be to flush the toilets. There is something uniquely unpleasant about facing two or three days of an unflushed toilet.

At least you can usually purchase fresh water for drinking. I say "usually" because it is amazing how fast Americans can get to their local stores when an emergency arises and how quickly the stores run out of bottled water. As soon as the weather forecaster mentions a storm, "And this is going to be a big one, folks, so stock up!" Americans will empty the grocery shelves of bread, canned tuna, toilet paper, and gallon jugs of water.

Four years working at a grocery store and during my years as a customer, I've never witnessed any episodes of customer sharing. Individuals who got to the store after the rush started usually left with no water. They looked at their neighbors who arrived earlier, and those shopping carts were full. And I never witnessed any sharing. Maybe the sharing happened later, out in the parking lot, but I doubt it.

Concerns about water are pervasive even in our country, blessed with fairly abundant water supplies. But I can understand the classic John Wayne movies when everyone's guns come out of their holsters during fights over water. We are lucky that people don't often wear their guns to the store.

The army's basic training is an intense two-month period, designed to turn raw recruits into soldiers who can survive difficult conditions. The process works pretty well. Marching everywhere was part of that training. When we had long hikes, and this was during the hot Missouri summer, we still only had one canteen each. There was plenty of water in the camp, but the army was teaching us that we may be in a situation where we have to ration our water, and we better know how. Maybe that's when I first learned not to take water for granted and that I might not always be able to turn on a faucet and get all the water I wanted.

That background explains how I looked at this latest water crisis. I was mostly concerned with finding water to drink and, understandably, to continue flushing our toilets. But I also wanted to watch how residents here reacted to the water shortage. You get some interesting and, at times, depressing insights into human behavior when you watch people in a crisis. Visualize a group of regular people in a theater watching *The Sound of Music*, a peaceful, soothing film with uplifting music and kids dancing in the street. Suddenly, a somber voice states over a loudspeaker, "There is a fire in the theater! Please get up from your seats, locate the nearest exit, and walk to the exit sign in an orderly fashion. There is no cause for panic!"

Good luck! Even with the assurance that there was no reason to panic, my bet is that people will coalesce into screaming mobs as they rush for the exits. Even the people inclined to be orderly about the evacuation will likely be swept up into a panic mood. And heaven help anyone needing assistance.

But from what I saw of our water crisis, the residents here responded well. At least no one got trampled. Americans love thinking they are stoic and love stories about how they always come together during times of crisis. But our history suggests otherwise.

Remember the toilet paper "shortage" years ago? Not the real one during COVID but the "accidental" one, after some offhanded remark during *The Tonight Show Starring Johnny Carson*. The subsequent run on toilet paper was almost unbelievable, except that it wasn't. I remember getting a call from my mother-in-law that we "should not worry" because she had plenty of toilet paper. When we stopped by their house, she had a hundred rolls on their basement shelves. This purchase was a fairly major financial investment, but they were quite proud of their stash.

You see similar reactions whenever there are shortages—or perceived shortages. Americans want to be sure they have enough. This selfishness is neither surprising nor objectionable, but I still get depressed about our national character when I watch commercials from an organization that makes and ships large quantities of dried food. Their implication during their presentation is that it is a good idea for Americans to hide freeze-dried food for "the emergency," as though they know something we don't. And they assure you that the food containers come to your door unmarked, presumably so your neighbors won't know you have extra food!

These examples are not meant to argue that Americans are

selfish, but a significant proportion of our country responds to such appeals. I don't think the desire to "take care of yourself" is a bad thing. But it does say something about us as a society. How many of the people who ordered unmarked food boxes will be willing to share if their neighbors are suffering during some prolonged emergency? It's better if we don't know.

Here is another assessment about our national character: I don't remember a recent disaster in this country where some looting did not emerge. Even the September 11 attack was not immune. One author described looting at the crash scenes, even by the first responders.

But I didn't see or hear objectionable or selfish actions during the water crisis here. One reason for the good behavior might be that everyone at The Home was, if I can use this example, in the same boat. If one section of the community had drinking water and showers while the rest were desperate enough to run through a car wash without their cars, then tempers would have flared. But they didn't, and so they didn't. And the administration had stocked up on bottled water, so drinking water was available. Some residents, though, were reluctant to go to the dining area to get drinking water because of their lack of showers.

As the days passed, we discovered that there were several intersecting problems with the water supply. It is so much easier to handle one problem. But if there are several, then fixing them is more difficult—something like working on a Rubik's Cube.

One element of our water problem involved the sprinkler system in one of the newer apartment buildings. It had ruptured. One resident said more than six thousand gallons of water went into the apartments. The problem with obtaining figures like that while standing in the parking lot is that you have no way to judge credibility. These figures, any figures, take on a life of their own, usually growing and changing as they are passed from one resident to another. So, a six-thousand-gallon leak in Building A becomes a twenty-thousand-gallon leak as the story is told and retold. The sprinkler problem was bad enough, but Asheville also picked this time to experience problems with one of its pumping stations. They had to cut water off from the entire south end of the city, and that is where we were.

The situation had its humorous aspects—if you are blessed with an unusual sense of humor. People were looking for water, but they were also looking for functioning toilets. When I went to the grocery store for bottled water, I was heartbroken to see a rope across the entrance to their restroom facilities. "Cleanup on aisle four" had an entirely new connotation for me.

The maintenance people here responded as well as they could; the crew made water available for toilet flushing. I hope that someone suggests they consider outdoor toilets should a similar emergency occur. Those portable sheds have their problems, but they are infinitely better than no toilets.

The overall atmosphere here was positive. The residents shared what they had, and the employees worked hard to ensure no one suffered more than necessary. I heard the occasional complaint—"There is no excuse for this water problem"—but similar complaints exist across the country whenever a problem emerges. I would enjoy asking the complaining parties how they voted the last time there was a bond issue to upgrade the city's water system—a bond issue that would have raised their property taxes.

If I were grading our retirement community on its response to the water crisis, I give it a B. I base the grade reduction on several things. My initial criticism concerns the absence of prompt and accurate information about both water problems. Most residents in this community are online, but the information flow through the internet was not particularly "timely." There were hours, sometimes days, when the community relied on word-of-mouth. An informal source might be better than no source, but it is no substitute for accurate information.

I understand there was a time when the community and city administrators had no idea what the problem was, how they would fix it, or how long it would take. And it turned out that as they were working on one problem, another problem emerged. Any individual who has worked on home plumbing can sympathize with serial plumbing problems.

Although the administration provided drinking water, the water to flush the toilets did not come until two days into the crisis. But residents had to bring containers and carry them to their homes or apartments. For some people, that task was difficult; for others, it was impossible. We hauled water to a few residents, but I suspect that many people confronted their unflushed home toilets for the entire week. Judging from the vacant stares when the topic comes up, some residents have yet to recover.

The last element in this complex water problem involved a valve. These simple devices are vital elements in any piping system, central to directing and controlling the flow of things like gas and water. I remember how often I found leaks in our Hampshire water system. The leak would be in our crawl space and almost always involved a valve. Wouldn't you think that a nation that could send people to the moon could come up with better valves? I have always enjoyed that phrase, illogical as it might be.

Anyway, for reasons that are still not clear, the valve controlling the water from the city system into our little community presented some continuing problems, and it remained a problem for more than a week after the other issues were resolved. If I were asked for advice from a young person who was undecided about what type of career she could pursue, one that offered a high degree of job security, I would have no hesitancy in suggesting that she "get into valves."

If Hollywood decides to remake *The Graduate*, and they seemed inclined to do such things, the older guy would be advising Benjamin to "get into valves" instead of plastic. Our country is always going to need valves, and if you can design a foolproof valve or find a way to repair existing valves without destroying the whole street, the world will beat a path to your door.

Returning to the water crisis here, a B is not a bad grade for our

community. And there is the attractive possibility of doing better \
next time. Because there will likely be a next time!

Dave:

It is New Year's Eve Eve, and I thought I might as well clean up, as it were, residual questions before starting the New Year with a clean slate. And speaking of "clean slates," I managed to negotiate a "bowel treaty" with Mery. She recently installed bamboo toilet paper in what she calls the "master bathroom," but I continue using my Charmin two-ply, aloe-scented paper in the secondary bathroom, the one nobody pays attention to, the one without matching towels.

You had a question about why we were going to Salisbury so often because Salisbury is not exactly a tourist mecca. Mery's brother lives there, and we have been doing his household chores once a month. After a few months, we decided to stay overnight in that bucolic town because the trip was long, almost three hours each way, and going back and forth was tiring. Staying over was a nice treat, a period of relaxation, that is until Mery discovered her "Quality Inn."

If you follow the news from Asheville, you know that we are finishing with an extended water crisis. Almost a week without any water, and our fellow residents did not look good after a few days. One lady explained to me, "I'm going to have to take a shower with a sandblaster."

The Home decided to start providing water for residents to flush their toilets, probably because the neighborhood smelled like Chicago's Back of the Yards in the 1950s. Finally, I found a use for those accursed frosting tubs, the ones Mery planned to use for the drum circle. Are you reading my emails, Dave? Do you remember any of my fascinating stories?

These plastic containers hold five gallons of water, which I could pour into the toilet tank.

Mery spread the word, and I hauled water tubs to various apartments to flush appliances that, by then, resembled Chicago's L-station toilets. Do you remember how bad those toilets were? Do such images stick in your mind the way they do mine?

Well, I think this cleans up (chuckle) the questions and issues so we can start the New Year fresh. Something like having a new roll of Charmin two-ply on my toilet roll. And so, Happy New Year! Keep me in your prayers. By the way, Dave, starting a daily prayer routine might be a good resolution for you.

Dan

9.

A Few More Thoughts About Life at *the Home!*

We are approaching the first anniversary of our move to this age-based, "everything is done for you so you can live the life you deserve" community. And my conclusion about the new lifestyle is that it is not nearly as negative as I thought it would be.

Was it Shakespeare who wrote that memorable line about "damning with faint praise?" Maybe it was Woody Allen. Whoever said it was onto something, the notion that even when we are praising someone or something, we might be disguising a few reservations. And I suppose that I am hiding a few reservations.

This recent move involved a change from a fairly secluded mountain home to a more communal-type life. We are now in a setting where we see people everywhere, sitting on one of the many benches, standing in clusters on the sidewalks and the dining room, parking their cars, and roaming the hallways, many of them poised for extended conversations about who knows what, and where they were when they found out what they knew. It is like living in one of those summer camps for kids, where everyone wanted to talk, except I never went to one of those camps, so how would I know?

This relocation was not an easy move for either of us, but I think that the process was more difficult for me. If there is a key to understanding the trauma that moving to one of the nation's retirement communities generates in many people, in me, for instance, and why I damned this new home with faint praise, the key is not so much the communal life with people standing everywhere but the traumatic realization that I am getting older. In the eyes of the world—and we have to be honest, those are important eyes—I am already old. Why else would I move to a retirement community?

That personal realization about being old means I am adjusting to more than people lurking outside our front door. I have to deal with me, or I should say the new and much older me! Some of the adjustments will be more difficult than others, but none will be easy. Being old is new to me and presumably to many of the other residents. I spent much of my academic career studying the aging process, looking at and talking with older people in a variety of settings. But when you are looking at your own life, at what you are doing and feeling and how you are reacting to unfamiliar terrain, it is a challenging process.

Sometime during the reflection process, I wondered if a noncredit course on trends in refrigerator magnets might be a good idea. That course probably has no direct connection to aging, but some potentially fascinating topics could lead into some useful discussions; for example, what are the most popular magnet sayings? How did the popularity of certain magnets change over time? Are the Mark Twain quotes still popular? How about Woody Allen? How many magnets do people here have on their refrigerators, and does this number differ by religious or ethnic grouping? How often do people change their magnets? Do people ever throw a magnet away, and if so, why?

One of my favorite magnets disappeared from our refrigerator door when we moved, and I haven't found out what happened to it. Not yet! Anyway, that provocative magnet stated, "I lived, I loved, I laughed! Now what?" I could not summarize the getting older process any better than that. Well, maybe I could, but I'll begin this overview with that quote.

A few generations ago, the old age threshold, the chronological point when society defined individuals as old, was sixty-five. Our country used that arbitrary age because it was the point when Americans became eligible for full social security benefits. And then many private organizations began using that age for their mandatory retirement points, and sixty-five became the almost universal point of transition into old age.

Social attitudes about old age are somewhat different now, partly because of increases in longevity. People in their sixties, seventies, and even eighties are writing books, performing on stages, jumping out of planes, going into space, and obviously running for public office. But no matter what Americans are doing, or not doing, few of us are happy with the "old" label. Old wine, old cheese, old dogs, old cars, and even old homes are fine, but old man or old lady, these categories still imply a lot of undesirable personal characteristics. If you ask young people what they visualize when they hear the term "old person," you hear descriptions like decline, infirm, incapacitated, wrinkled—nothing positive. Bernard Baruch had a great answer to that question about whether he was old. He was in his nineties when he said that old age "was ten years older than I am."

As individuals, we can take a more positive approach to the notion of being old; "To hell with them and what they think. It only matters what I think and how old I feel." And we may believe that. But part of what we confront with our advancing age, in addition to our own feelings, are the negative attitudes from the community. No matter how much we say we don't care, it is difficult to ignore your neighbor's, your coworkers', and even your family's attitudes.

I suspect that this might be one of the reasons many older Americans elect to move to one of the nation's retirement communities. No one forced them, at least not directly; they came to a retirement community, as we did, because it represents an appealing lifestyle. And many older Americans apparently like the idea of living with other people their age.

I noticed in the resident profiles here that a high proportion of residents moved to this community to be closer to their families because they liked the mountains or were tired of maintaining a home. No one stated that they wanted to be with people their own age. They may not even realize how important it is to live around individuals in their age group. But it is tiring, trying to keep up with friends and neighbors much younger than you are.

This community's residents are active. They may slow down, but they participate in their world. Residents attend local activities and musical events and pack the community room for the various events that are held. A significant number are also working and volunteering in the outside community. Many of them got involved in the recent election, working as poll watchers or election judges and even going door-to-door for their candidates.

A few weeks ago, I was talking about participation in our community's spectrum of activities with my cluster representative, who, not incidentally, is my wife. I spend more time with my cluster representative than most residents. I told her I saw nothing wrong with her urging residents to get more involved in activities as long as there was no pressure. Drawing on my sociology background, which sometimes comes in handy, I explained that even subtle pressures can be overwhelming, and you have to be careful about urging residents too hard. The almost instinctive desire to be part of a group, or at least not to be weeded out of one, can overwhelm a person's preference to be left alone.

I used social drinking as an example, although it may not be a perfect one. Perfect examples of anything are not easy to find, and when you write a long essay or, in this case, a book, you use whatever pops into your mind. That is fine, as long as the connection is not obscure. Anyway, the process that occurs when many of us began our social drinking and smoking is a good example of the influence that social pressure can have. Our immersion into alcohol and tobacco was dictated by the almost universal youthful need to "fit in," to be accepted into groups that spend a portion of their time drinking and smoking. Because it was the "in" thing.

I've never met anyone who enjoyed their first beer, their initial taste of whiskey, or their initial attempt with inhaling or, heaven forbid, chewing tobacco. Consumptions of these addictive and often unpleasant products are learned tastes. It's nothing like the first pleasurable experience of a cookie from Grandma's oven or your first taste of apple pie sprinkled with cinnamon. I remember some guys in the service who smoked because they felt as though they had to if they wanted to be part of the group. They smoked their cigarettes without inhaling, and it was kind of sad, for me at least, to watch them blowing out those puffs of smoke.

Many of us began our use of tobacco or alcohol in someone else's basement or, more likely, in someone's car. Some guy took his father's cigarettes, someone else grabbed a few beers from the family refrigerator, and there we were, with beer and cigarettes. We took those first unpleasant drinks or puffs because of the social pressure because everyone else was doing it. We needed to belong and be one of the guys or girls. We ignored the bad tastes in our mouths that lasted for hours and didn't stop to think that maybe others in the group, maybe all of them, had the same feelings. We started on a path of addiction that we should never have walked, not at the tender ages we did. And getting on those paths was a lot easier than getting off!

Taking those initial puffs or sips seems almost idiotic now when we have the luxury of looking back. But it didn't just seem an idiotic thing to do; it was idiotic, and there is no other way to describe it. When we look back and see ourselves learning to like, or trying our best to like, drinking and smoking because it seemed important to fit in, to finally be adults, we have to shake our heads. We despair about the stupidity of young people today who get rushed to hospitals because of some ritual-induced binge drinking, and we forget about our own stupid episodes.

We wonder now what the hell we were thinking, trying so hard to fit into social groups we may not have enjoyed anyway. But that is part of the learning curve, recognizing that this need to fit in is sometimes necessary, occasionally appropriate, but not always the best road. Sometimes, it is better not to fit in, but it takes time to learn that lesson. Fitting in and going with the flow—this is the preferred American way of life. To get along, you have to go along. Going along was even more important when you were younger, but that pressure to conform doesn't disappear after graduation. Depending on where you are and who you are, fitting in may continue to be one of your life's major components.

🏠🏠🏠

But this conformity comes with a personal cost. You discover that you are frequently in social situations you don't enjoy, with people you may not like, and engaged in activities you would not ordinarily select. This pressure to conform can be a positive process. Group conformity produces cohesion and provides group stability. On the other hand—and doesn't there always seem to be another hand—fitting in can be a negative process that inhibits individual initiative and personal satisfaction. "The nail that sticks up the highest gets hammered down" is a Japanese proverb that has always been one of my favorite refrigerator magnets.

As we approach the latter stage of life, we may not even know what we want to do or if there is anything we really want to do because, in our long and sometimes tortuous history of conforming, we don't always ask ourselves what we feel like doing; instead, we wonder and even worry about what our friends and neighbors want us to do.

And that was the point I tried to make to my cluster representative—if she was still listening. You should be careful, I said, walking that fine line between pressuring and encouraging. At this stage in people's lives, individuals are entitled to live not only the life they deserve but the life they want!

Some of us, maybe most of us, still aren't sure what the hell we want. We have walked in someone else's parade for so long that we may not be confident marching alone. And maybe we are still not sure where we want to go. Maybe we still need to hear someone else's drum. I can't help thinking that this is a sad picture, a person arriving at life's final stage and ready to live the life she deserves, but having no idea what that life should be. Or what she deserves!

Besides watching for conformity pressures, I kept looking for any evidence of another interesting social process. One of the interesting things that emerges in and around social groups involves *labeling*. Labels, who uses them and what happens when they are applied, can be fascinating. Labels are like personal stickers that tell the world who people are. Not always who they think they are but who others think they are! And there can be profound differences there. Something like a label on a dented can indicating canned carrots, but when you get home and open the can, you find creamed corn.

You can't see the social labels. But the labels are there, and unlike paper labels, social labels tend to stick. A label on a person given to them in high school can remain through adulthood. And with the influence of today's social media, anyone can attach a label. I just finished reading an article documenting the millions of dollars the Chinese government spends every year spewing out poisonous comments about any American who has been critical of China. That kind of destructive power, once the sole province of influential people like newspaper editors, political leaders, and ministers, is now wielded by anyone with a computer.

At one time, I would have put barbers on that list of influential people. You may have read how influential barbers have been in the past when the barber shop was often the primary meeting place for community leaders. When we first moved to Asheville, North Carolina, I started going to a barber who seemed to have contacts everywhere. He knew what was going on in the city, what was happening in our quiet neighborhood, and not incidentally, he was a great barber.

When I mentioned that "some of us were wondering" (a phrase I use when I really mean, "I was wondering") what would happen with the empty lot on the corner, down from the barbershop, my barber assured me, with the classic wink and nod, "I've been told that they are putting a grocery store in there."

That was welcome news to an area devoid of grocery stores, and I spread the word far and wide in my neighborhood. Or as far and wide as you can in a small neighborhood of fifteen homes. When the grocery store failed to materialize, my standing as a source of good information took a major hit. "Why don't you ask your barber?" became the mantra of my caustic neighbors. And for the record, in case anyone keeps tabs on such things, that empty lot is still empty.

Returning to the labeling process, labels can be positive or negative, although the negative labels seem to be more persistent. Parents, for example, are generous in describing their children as geniuses, or perhaps just gifted, but those positive labels peel off fast, especially if the gifted kid flunked out of three universities. The more destructive labels, such as being slow or antisocial, can be a problem for the rest of that child's life. Later in life, labels of ex-convict, mental patient, or violent can put individuals into impossible situations.

When Europeans first invaded this continent, they were fairly strict in enforcing the prevailing values, especially if they resided in permanent settlements. Hawthorne's classic, *The Scarlet Letter*, graphically described how labeling worked. Poor Hester Prynne violated the group's sexual norms, and she paid a heavy price. Back then, the offending individual, usually female, had to wear the letter "A" on her dress if the community authorities considered her guilty of adultery. The label was a badge of dishonor, a label the entire community could see every day. And the responses involved everything from shunning to physical punishments.

We are more enlightened now. You don't have to wear any letters on your shirt, but we still have the courts and our neighbors who will attach the labels. And you don't always need a formal court to "convict." All it takes is a Facebook post and followers. A negative newspaper article can also be effective, at least within the decreasing pool of Americans who read their daily papers.

How does the labeling process work? Let's say that Frank (not his real name) was convicted of marijuana possession, and the court sentenced him to three years in jail. That lengthy sentence for what sociologists describe as a "victimless crime" seems excessive, but even longer sentences for minor offenses have been imposed in recent years. All part of the "get tough on crime" philosophy that, sadly, has not yet run its course. And so, the hypothetical Frank goes to the slammer.

When Frank is released, assuming he didn't get into more trouble in prison, he arrives home with two labels—ex-convict and drug offender. It will be hard for a guy to get a decent job, and having both of those negative labels will probably doom any attempt he makes to carve out a successful life. Poor Frank, despite what might be considerable talents, is stuck with two negative labels. There is no "label appeal," and the unforgiving world is going to make the rest of Frank's life more difficult.

Negative labels might be completely unreasonable, but "reason" often gets lost or ignored. A man recently had to register as a "sex offender" because he was guilty of having sex with a minor. That crime seems worthy of contempt. As it turns out, that minor was his sixteen-year-old girlfriend; the offender was eighteen at the time of the offense, an adult according to the law, but his girlfriend was not. The guy was found guilty and spent time in jail, and he now has that label. When he moves to a new community, his neighbors will discover that their new resident is a "registered sex offender." Not incidentally, that sex offender married his girlfriend after she turned eighteen. In the long run, maybe everything will turn out fine for them. But I doubt it.

I remember the reaction of an individual who, when he read about a man recently acquitted of murder in a jury trial, said, "Well,

I'm sure he was guilty of something. Otherwise, they wouldn't have charged him." The legal perspective that you are innocent until proven guilty does not always apply to labeling.

Years ago, I wanted to illustrate how labeling worked, so I conducted a minor experiment in my social issues class. It didn't turn out the way I hoped. After I explained what labeling meant and discussed its implications, I pointed out a member of the class, at random, but the poor guy was sitting in front of the class and was an easy target. This, by the way, is another example of why, back when I was taking classes in school, I never sat in the front row. You are too easy a target when you sit in front of a room.

I told the class that the student I pointed to had recently been released from a mental hospital, but he is fine now, and the "mental patient" label should not be part of anyone's feelings about him. Individuals should be judged by what they do, and not because of a negative label. We talked about the problems that a mental patient label could generate, how everything the poor guy did would be filtered through that label. I even pointed to the student in the front row a few more times and made comments like, "Joe probably chews on his pencil the way he is doing now because they never permitted pencils in the institution, and he can't get used to using one."

After a few more illustrations, I finally told the class that I made up that mental hospital confinement, that Joe was as normal as anyone else in the class and was never in a mental institution. I could see the suspicious looks on some faces. They did not believe my disclaimer, and from what Joe told me at the end of the semester, he never overcame my hypothetical "label." Joe told me the other students never reacted to him in the same way. He was bothered because it affected his potential relationship with a certain female student.

I explained that some of that perceived reaction might be his own sensitivities, that because of the experiment, he was far more sensitive to the feelings and perceptions of other people. I said that was maybe one good thing to come from the episode. I don't think he believed me. I'm not sure I even believed what I was telling him, and I never tried anything like that again.

That labeling process was in my mind during a meeting our building had with the social worker. I never had a social worker assigned to me, and I admit it was an unsettling experience. I didn't think I needed a social worker. I have never needed a social worker, and I didn't want a social worker right then. I was imagining a meeting this guy might have with his colleagues, when I would be described as "a paranoid resident" because of my unreasonable apprehension about social workers.

In that meeting, the social worker provided us, his assigned clients, with a comprehensive overview of his responsibilities. He urged us to be alert for any signs of dementia in our fellow residents. "Dementia" is another interesting, negative label, a catch-all term applied almost exclusively to older people. This label encompasses virtually anything a person does that falls into the category of "unusual behavior." But unusual behavior is another broad category, difficult to define and certainly hard to measure.

I have been at Elks Club meetings where you could describe almost all the social behavior as "unusual." And have you ever watched the behavior of football fans following the big game at a local sports bar? As far as I know, which may not be that far anymore, medical professionals don't use "dementia" as often as they once did because "unusual" behavior is difficult to define and even more difficult to measure. But that is another unfortunate characteristic of labels. Even if they are vague, once they are out there, they tend to persist, like bad colds or bad movies.

"Be sure to let me know," the social worker told us when he stood up to leave, and he sounded somber. "If your neighbor is walking around doing something unusual, like wearing inappropriate clothing... and if you see any unusual behavior, call me!"

I chuckled, but I did it quietly because I wasn't going to let anyone hear me. I'm sure that someone would have considered my laugh unusual and flagged down the social worker.

That inappropriate clothing description pretty much describes me. I have this pair of jeans that are like an old friend. They have a few rips, maybe more than a few, but that description puts me in style. People now pay big money for new clothes that have attractive rips. And I have a couple of really comfortable T-shirts with paint stains. Those stains are good memories of successful painting jobs. But I can foresee a few residents telephoning the social worker, concerned about how I am walking around in rags.

I am not going to be surprised if I get a call from him, telling me that he would like to stop by for a chat. And when he does, I am sure he will mention my clothing. When I explain that I feel comfortable in my clothes, his written notes that will doubtlessly wind their way into a computerized file will state, "Resident doesn't seem to understand how inappropriate his clothing choices are and how his choice of clothing bothers the neighbors. Everyone seems worried about him. The situation bears watching."

I don't want to suggest that labeling is running amok in this or any other retirement community, but running amok is certainly a possibility. Because Americans tend to attach labels to people or groups with reckless abandon, and retirement communities are not immune to that tendency. Especially if they have practiced it throughout their lives. Maybe it was my imagination—my imagination does wander in unusual directions on occasion—but I thought I caught a few suspicious glances in my direction after the social worker left.

Any lapse in memory, act of forgetting, locking yourself out of your apartment, which, by the way, is surprisingly easy to do if you haven't lived in an apartment in years, or having tremors in your hands when you eat dinner because you had too many Moscow Mules the night before can have your neighbors wondering whether you might have Parkinson's (a currently popular affliction) or are exhibiting the initial states of dementia (whatever they might be).

And all it takes for a label to be affixed to your forehead, figuratively speaking, is for one person to make the designation. The local grapevine does the rest. You will be wearing a virtual scarlet letter on your paint-stained shirt. Somewhere, Hester Prynne is smiling.

And medical labels are a separate category of negative labels. If your hands shake when you eat dinner, you will see heads turn in your direction. Heads turn here often, and the informal and erroneous diagnoses of Parkinson's can spread around before everyone finishes their dinners. The informal diagnostic process here is comparable to a pattern seen in medical schools. The "intern syndrome" occurs when medical students think they have the disease they are currently studying. The students hear about a disease in class, read about it in their textbooks, discuss it at length in study groups, and dissect the body of a man who died from that disease. Now some of the students are sure they have that dreaded disease.

In our community, there is a process I would term a "retirement community syndrome." RCS exists when you think someone else has the disease you read about on the internet, that you heard about on a television talk show, or you know the signs because your neighbor years ago died from it. Like in medical schools, you expect that this syndrome is more silly than serious in its implications.

So much for labeling. What about death and dying? Some of us remember that spate of songs in the 1950s, with teenagers getting run over by trains after going back for their boyfriend's high school ring or kids jumping off a bridge because the other kids made fun of their clothing. Nothing like listening to the oldies and goodies for that rush of good feelings!

But after you get older, the topics become a little more urgent. I asked a nursing home administrator years ago why his institution did not provide any resident training sessions about illness and death. You don't get into your seventies and beyond without thinking about your own or your neighbor's mortality. Americans often avoid difficult topics though, and death and dying are not comfortable discussions. This administrator told me that they stayed away from the topics because "it depresses people." I asked how they handled the situation when one of their residents died, and he told me they ignored it. "We don't pick up the body until late at night when everyone is sleeping. Then we remove it, empty the apartment or room, and the next day, everyone goes on with their daily routines."

And what about the memories of the person who died? "No one mentions his name, at least the staff doesn't. I'm not sure if the residents do. But we try to discourage any discussions about the person or his death. It is best for everyone."

Fortunately, there is more of a willingness to discuss death and dying in the country now, and that trend seems true here at The Home too. The publication that the campus issues on a biweekly basis lists residents who died during the previous period, occasionally with some biographical information. Judging from the obits, we have four or five deaths a month in the community. I have not seen any bodies being taken from the buildings, but I am watching. Not all the time, but I am on alert whenever I see an ambulance going down the road.

Speaking of death, I thought about suggesting a seminar on "last words and actions." The initial questions to the people who enrolled would be *What do you want your friends, relatives, and neighbors to remember about you? Are there a few "final words" that might make your family smile, despite your departure?*

I love the last words of Oscar Wilde: "Either this wallpaper goes or I do." And I enjoyed reading the last words of the French poet, Paul Claudel. Actually, he asked a question. "Doctor, do you think it could have been the sausage?"

If Paul had eaten my grandmother's sausage—actually, if he had ever eaten pretty much anything at my grandmother's table—the experience could have been his undoing. I am not saying that my grandmother's cooking would kill you, but I can guarantee you would not feel better afterward.

I am always surprised at the proportion of people who gush about their grandmother's cooking. And they will inevitably praise her baking as well, proclaiming, "No one bakes cinnamon rolls like my grandmother!" You get the idea that learning to bake perfect bread and cinnamon rolls is part of the transition to becoming a grandmother.

When I was in the army, the emotions about not being home for Christmas were sometimes overwhelming. The base theater always showed a sappy holiday movie, something like *Christmas in Connecticut* or *White Christmas*, and at the film's end, there wouldn't be a dry eye anywhere. Now, did all of us, or did *any of us*, have home lives like that bucolic family in Connecticut? I doubt it. And just as very few soldiers had ideal home lives, I think it is equally unlikely that so many grandmas were such marvelous cooks.

My grandmother made apple sauce. She had two apple trees in her yard that provided a steady supply, at least during the summer and fall, but the thought of my grandmother's apple sauce brings tears to my eyes, not a smile to my face. Eating Grandma's concoctions could, and did once or twice, induce choking.

Her apple sauce had the consistency, and occasionally the taste, of industrial putty. Grandma did not worry about what most good cooks considered routine procedures, like seed removal, separating the good from the rotten apples, and using either brown or white sugar to sweeten the taste. Actually, I never saw any sugar of any type in her kitchen, and I'm not sure she would have used it if someone brought over a bag.

I remember watching my grandmother throw the good and not-so-good apples from her trees into a large metal washtub and mash the ingredients, using an implement that resembled a garden rake. I think she used the rake for other things, like cleaning the chicken coop, but this is only a suspicion. And I never saw her washing the apples. I would like to say she stirred the mix until it reached a smooth consistency, but the stirring only continued until Grandma got tired. After she was tired, she spooned the gooey mix into her collection of old jars, screwed the lids on, and set them on a basement shelf where they stood until the next family meal.

Enough about my grandmother's culinary skills. But I have seen enough to make a general statement; getting older is no guarantee that your cooking and baking skills are going to improve. I think you could make a more compelling argument that cooking skills diminish as you age because of the significant decline in our senses of smell and taste.

Back to the prospect of people's last words. I think a "last words seminar" could be an especially interesting and productive session. We could set up a website (www.myfinalthoughts.com?) for storing everyone's last words, and relatives could click on it whenever they were nostalgic. Maybe on a night when they started thinking about a favorite and now deceased uncle. Or years later when they are having their own end-of-life reflections.

All things considered, which they rarely are, it may be a good thing that people do not dwell on their life's final moments. It could easily become an obsession. It might not be best to describe the seminar as a means of selecting your last words because we don't usually know when our time is going to be up. It's not like a commuter train pulling out of the station at exactly 3:10. Although American trains do not have the reputation of leaving on time.

It might be better if we talked about this proposed seminar as having an opportunity to compose a few final thoughts. I think people would be comfortable with that idea, knowing that they didn't have to keep some pithy final quote in their mind, ready to spout when they thought the end was near. Because there are going to be false alarms, and you don't want to recite your rehearsed final words and then have the doctor say, "Oh, stop babbling; you're going to be fine. It's just indigestion. Have you been eating that homemade apple sauce again?"

Now you are going to have to come up with a whole new "final words" statement. If you decide to use the same statement again because you thought it was so memorable, your final words could end up being given the same status as Tom Brady's retirement announcement.

As long I am on the topics of death and dying, we recently arranged our "earth-friendly" burials. It is nice that our environmental concerns will be apparent right up to that last shovel of dirt being thrown on our degradable burial boxes. During the burial discussion, the funeral director asked for our address. He needed to know where he would have to pick up the body. I wondered at the time, *Do you ever get used to that question when it applies to you?* I know I'm not used to it. When we gave him the address, he nodded and said, "Yes, we have a lot of business from the residents there."

I don't think I would have had the same uneasy feeling if we had been talking to a furniture salesman, but this guy was not selling furniture. This personal discomfort during the session with the funeral director suggests another explanation for my lingering unease with this move to a retirement community. I understand that I am closing out my life cycle, clearing out my psychological cabinets, and preparing for the ultimate going-out-of-business sale. I suppose I am thinking that people are thinking what I was thinking when I found out that an individual was headed for a retirement community.

In years past, when someone told me about such a move, I had this vision of an elephant plodding his way toward his eventual and inevitable demise, a death migration on a road paved by generations of genes. But it does not matter what I am thinking; it is what the rest of the world is thinking. And what they are thinking involves the label that may be on the whole community where we now reside. Someone once described a city in Florida, maybe it was St. Petersburg, as "death's waiting room." The waiting room label was now in the back of my mind.

Residents here are approaching the end of their life cycles, and as with individuals in retirement communities throughout the country, they have made their way to a place of comfort where, like our *Loxodonta africana* relatives, they are getting ready to die. In a sense, we are all unconsciously walking toward our burial grounds. I don't mean or regard this as morbid, but that image may explain my persistent and perhaps unconscious psychological discomfort with the drastic turn in my life.

So, have I answered the questions I posed at the start of this book? I asked one central question: is retirement housing a good idea? Before moving here, I thought that age-segregated housing made good sense, and now that we have been here for a year, I still think so.

Older Americans seem comfortable with all their neighbors in the same age category. We don't need to conduct polls about this; older Americans have been voting with their pocketbooks and their moving vans. There are currently more than five thousand retirement communities in the country, and that number seems certain to grow.

Does this movement weaken the social structure of younger communities? That depends on how we choose to define "weaken." It means that a young family cannot go across the street to seek the advice of an older neighbor, but how often do such cross-generational queries happen anyway?

Now that I have time for research—living the life people say we deserve—I will try looking at some other intriguing questions, like those involving refrigerator magnets. I no longer worry about shoveling the driveway, raking the lawn, cleaning the gutters, washing the windows, or painting the house. On the other hand, I think about my emerging irrelevance, possible dementia, torn clothing, and muscle aches. And, of course, there is that burial plot with my name on it.

All this may be yet another example of the yin-yang principle, a universal process that maintains harmony in the universe. We give a little, and we get a little. It all balances in the end.

And that is a nice thought.

Dave:

We are amid an "endless whirl" of holiday social activities. You might think that *The Home* would have one holiday party, probably with alcohol-free punch and store cookies, and everyone would be home by eight to watch *Miracle on 34th Street*, the one with Natalie Wood. Well, you would be wrong. Not completely wrong, but somewhat. Mostly!

Not a day goes by that we do not receive an email invitation to yet another "holiday extravaganza" from groups you might not think would be interested in holding a party. Or inviting us. But they are. And they did. In just the last week, we have received invitations to:

1. The campus holiday gathering.
1. The campus formal preconcert taste centers (formal dress encouraged but not required.) What are your feelings when you get an invitation like this, Dave? Are you going to wear formal dress? Do you even have formal dress? Do you know precisely what it entails?
1. The building party. (Everyone in the building is invited to attend!) Please bring chairs and alcoholic drinks. Who knows what will happen when the wine spritzers start to flow?
1. The Dulcimer party. (I believe this party was restricted to the members of the Dulcimer Club. And yes, there is such a club, and they have regular meetings, with minutes.)
1. The cluster party. (They ask that you please sign up for the snack you want to bring.)
1. The Line Dancer party.

And there may be more because no group wants to be left off the "Wow, what a great party!" list. Mery's drum circle was thinking of having a party until I pointed out that there are currently only three active people in that group. I was one of the three, and I would not attend any party of three people. Even if we are all going to whack our drums.

On a more positive note, I think I may have told you that we have selected our gravesites, and I am not exaggerating when I say that we gave that decision more consideration than we gave to some of our home purchases. We selected a "green cemetery" that ensures our remains will not cause problems for the earth. I guess this makes up for all the problems I caused while I walked around. (Ha, ha!)

Parenthetically, Dave, Cassie, who administers the cemetery affairs, is an interesting and attractive young woman. I mention that because I expected the graveyard supervisor to look something like Lon Chaney Jr. Do you remember him, Dave? No one ever played the Wolf Man better than Lon Chaney Jr. And Lon would have been a great gravesite guide, but if Lon handled things, I think you would want to do your tour during daylight hours.

Anyway, the attractive Cassie took us on the tour; she showed us the available "housing sites" and was excited when we paid for them right away. No sense waiting for the after-holiday rush. Cassie apparently has been fascinated by graveyards since high school and loves her job. Two days ago, we received an email from her welcoming us as the newest "guests" at the Carolina Memorial Sanctuary.

At least I won't have to worry about the quality of the food after being buried there. At least, I don't think I will. Well, assuming you already have your chestnuts roasting on an open fire, I hope you have a relaxing holiday season.

And maybe you can block out a few hours to catch the Boris Karloff Christmas movie festival. It's bound to be better than watching *It's A Wonderful Life* yet again. I'm trying to find something that would be worse than watching that Jimmy Stewart movie again. But I can't.

Dan

David:

   I would love to say that picturing you laying on a white sandy beach, sipping an iced lime vodka while watching the nubile Latin beauties playing beach volleyball while I sit in our tiny apartment, watching residents navigate their walkers on their way down to our institutional restaurant for the "Italian chicken over balsamic rice" doesn't bother me. But I would be lying.

   It's not fair, but then, when has life ever been fair? Was it fair that you were in a volleyball class at Navy Pier while I got the shit beat out of me in boxing class? Was it fair that you were selling encyclopedias and sipping mixed drinks in a downtown Elburn bar while I unloaded food trucks in a dangerous Chicago South Side neighborhood?

   Believe it or not, and you probably won't, you cynical prick, we are getting acclimated to our retirement village. Mery more than me! She is going to meetings nonstop. Tomorrow, she goes to a meeting, and I swear I am not making this up, to assess how the other meetings are going. Apparently, the goal of this "meeting about meetings" is to decide—are you ready for this—if the resident association "needs more committee meetings in order to be more effective"! My question is "Can you imagine being less effective?"

   There was a "get acquainted" party last night in the community's restaurant arena. They hired a new chef, trained in food preparation and a veteran of kitchens from Schaumburg to Galesburg. They served four or five hors d'oeuvres, and if you had received any of these delicacies from one of those unsanitary food trucks you love, you would have kicked the truck tires in despair at the unpleasant taste. When someone observed that I had not eaten mine, and many residents here have this irritating tendency to look at what is happening on other people's plates, they asked if something was wrong, that I had not eaten all the wonderful items prepared by the new chef.

Mery, defending me in her unique way, which is sometimes more like a prosecutor than a defense attorney, said, "You have to ignore the amount of food he throws away because he doesn't like anything." Some great defense, huh, Dave? Right out of *My Cousin Vinny*!

I have started work on another book, this one centering on my first impressions of "The Home." Mery is concerned that the book might affect her standing in the community, but I assured her that the likelihood of it being published is about the same as my winning the lottery. And besides, I might be dead before the book appears in print. That prospect seemed to make her feel better.

Mery is leaving on a three-day trip to visit a friend who had the locker next to her in high school, and no, I am not making that up. She has remained friends with this person, and wouldn't you know it, this friend ended up living just a few hours away. Don't forget, Dave, the immortal words from Aristotle–governments are temporary, but locker mates are forever.

Well, I want to watch the Ping-Pong matches, and you probably want to start watching that volleyball game. I have to say this again: life just isn't fair.

Dan

Acknowledgments

Publishing a book is much easier when you have competent people helping to smooth out the rough spots. The professionals at Koehler Books were incredible: Miranda Dillon did a careful and effective editing of the book, Catherine Herold designed a perfect book cover, and Adrienne Folkerts capped the review process by incorporating everything done earlier—including my urgent last-minute changes. My thanks to all of them.

I also want to acknowledge the people who read an earlier draft and were gracious with their comments and suggestions. That reader list includes Gail Frey, Janet Aggen, Dr. David Edelberg, David Countryman, Irene Frederick, Diane Sanders, Joann Lausier, and Dr. Bryson Fretwell!

A few reviewers commented on the book title and wondered whether I would describe myself as "a classic car." It was a fair question, and I decided, after a short period of reflection, that I consider myself more of a dented can. David Edelberg mentioned during his review that all older Americans were dented cans. His analysis might be too severe an assessment of contemporary America, but maybe not.

When I read the reviews and thought again about the broader subject of getting older in our sometimes-fractured society, for some reason, I remembered the daily pronouncements by the legendary journalist and broadcaster Walter Cronkite; for those not old enough to remember that influential newsman, Walter usually wrapped up his nightly broadcasts by saying, "And that's the way it is." I wondered if he would be as calm if he still presented the nightly news now; would he gather the papers on his desk, inform his audience of David Edelberg's negative assessment about getting older, and then, in his careful tone, sign off, as always, "And that's the way it is!" I don't know about anyone else, but I miss Walter.

And finally, a major shout-out to my wife, Mery, who managed to read through a draft of the book without protesting the caustic discussions of our furniture shopping and her mother's china.

www.ingramcontent.com/pod-product-compliance
Lightning Source LLC
LaVergne TN
LVHW041948070526
838199LV00051BA/2942